Liturgy Coming to Life

By

JOHN A. T. ROBINSON

Bishop of Woolwich
Formerly Dean of Clare College, Cambridge

LONDON
A. R. MOWBRAY & Co. Limited

First published 1960
Second edition 1963
Second impression 1964

PRINTED IN GREAT BRITAIN BY
LOWE & BRYDONE (PRINTERS) LTD., LONDON

PREFACE TO THE SECOND EDITION

THIS book, first published in 1960, is an account of liturgical experiment at Clare College, Cambridge, of which I was privileged to be Dean from 1951 to 1959. It seeks to describe how liturgy can come to life in both senses, so that the Holy Communion may occupy its central and creative position in the common life of a community.

I have left the text as it stands despite the fact that the liturgical revival has moved on considerably in the past ten years. If one were starting afresh now one could doubtless afford to be bolder and more radical. But to presuppose the situation of the nineteen-fifties may help those who in most places are compelled to start a good deal further back still.

In retrospect I would say three things.

(1) I am still convinced that the place to begin is with bringing out the meaning of what is done rather than with changing what is said. Clothing the action with the right words is indeed of vital importance, when we know what we want to express. We need new and experimental liturgies alongside the old (not replacing it, any more than *The New English Bible* sets out to replace the Authorized Version of 1611). And, for the statutory services, we need revision of the old, conservatively and lovingly undertaken.[1] But no revision that has to command a two-thirds majority in Convocation and Church Assembly *even for experimental use* is likely to be very revolutionary. For some time to come, therefore, practical liturgical reform will have to be channelled into making the best of our late medieval (even if reformed) rite. And that may not be a bad thing. For at least it has the advantage of focusing attention on the heart of the matter, which in liturgy is something done rather than something said.

I have spoken in what follows of how the whole impact of the service can be transformed without altering a single prayer. There are, of course, many other ways of doing it

---

[1] I would commend to the Liturgical Commission the wisdom of the Church of India, Pakistan, Burma and Ceylon in sponsoring in its new Prayer Book *both* a revision of the traditional rite *and* a much more radical 'Liturgy for India'. There is surely a place for an order organically related to Cranmer's service and for an experimental liturgy for England in the second half of the twentieth century.

than those which we followed. I will not go into further detail. But as a result of recent experience I should like to commend (without any authority) the difference that comes over the service if the setting apart of the bread and wine is delayed until the beginning of the Eucharistic dialogue. The liturgy of the Word then runs straight on without a break from the sermon, notices and biddings into the intercession and communion preparation. *Then* if the offertory hymn is sung and the bread and wine brought up, the four-fold action of the Eucharist follows swiftly, compactly and without interruption. There is indeed also much to be said for this whole central part of the action, from the *Sursum Corda* to Communion, being taken standing. Even the prayer of humble access if it is said corporately and upstanding does not then appear the interruption that it must otherwise seem to the act of Thanksgiving.

But I am primarily concerned with making sense of what is ordinarily done. And the last thing I want to see is a new 'use', which suggests that there is a 'correct' way of doing things. Within the pattern set by the action itself I would plead for the maximum flexibility and adaptability. Indeed, in our liturgical situation, the way in which things are done allows scope for much more freedom and extemporization than what is said. It *should* differ with time and place and with the level or style of the Meal. What is appropriate in the house church or to the particular occasion will not necessarily be appropriate to the Cathedral celebration or to regular use. What is required above all is imagination and a feel for what is honest and genuinely expressive in *that* situation. I should be dismayed to hear of any church copying the order described in this book—though I am happy that the Communion Manual with which it closes has by now propagated quite a brood of children with recognizable family likeness.

Local experiment is vital—by which I mean corporate experiment by the whole people of God, including the bishop (as the president of every eucharist in his diocese) and in many cases also the architect. So much can be set in motion in the life of a community by people and priest taking trouble *together* over their liturgy. For, as Peter Hammond has said,[1]

---

[1] *Liturgy and Architecture* (1960), pp. 168 f.

'Liturgy is normative of ministry. . . . A clericalized liturgy means a clericalized apostolate. If, on the other hand, the layman has learned to accept his responsibilities as a member of an organic, priestly community, and as an active participant in the Eucharist, this awareness will undoubtedly be reflected in due course in his attitude towards the Church and its apostolic mission in the contemporary world. . . . The surest way of bringing home to the laity that they *are* the Church— and not the passive recipients of spiritual consolation at the hands of a professional ministry—is to make plain the full implications of the eucharistic liturgy'. And he goes on in words I would fully endorse from experience, 'It is a sheer waste of time to encourage the laity to co-operate with the clergy in teaching and evangelizing and to realize that they too are apostles, so long as we go on building [and, he would add, not adapting[1]] churches which make it virtually impossible for the ordinary Christian to play his full part in the very action which will inevitably be normative of his understanding of his mission'.

(2) Nothing I have said will, I trust, give the impression that I am unconvinced of the vital role of liturgy. But I must also confess to being increasingly conscious of the danger of liturgical revival for its own sake.

Liturgical action is symbolic, but if it becomes merely symbolic it simply succeeds in creating an artificial world of its own. It can so easily become theatre, with no real connections with the ongoing world outside. (For this reason I think I should now be more chary of the metaphor of the drama which runs through the Communion Addresses printed in the second section of the book.) And the *better* it is as theatre, the more successful a substitute it can become for real life. The more dynamically it speaks of action, of society, of matter, the more it can persuade people that they have 'engaged' when in fact they have done nothing. A liturgically trained congregation can actually be inoculated against genuine political and social involvement by being caught up in a pseudo-world of dramatic representation in which all the right motions—and emotions—are gone through. As Eric James has put it, 'The great danger is that Liturgy creates

[1] Cf. *Making the Building Serve the Liturgy* (ed. G. Cope), 1962.

a sacred world of things over against the secular, instead of a vision of the sacredness of the secular'.

These words come from his pamphlet, *The Roots of the Liturgy*,[1] whose insistence throughout is that 'the roots of the Liturgy are in the ground of society'.[2] But too often liturgy is a pot-plant, set in the glass-house of the sanctuary, whose roots are cut off from any direct connection with the soil of secular life. Indeed, one often gets the impression that unless this break were maintained the impact of the holy on the common would become unbearable. The *unconditional* sharing of bread and partaking of the common cup without any reservation would be insupportable unless it applied (seriously) only to this bread and this cup. If we are honest, we are all guilty of sustaining this demarcation; and the removal of our defences at this point can be shattering. It sets up reactions that remind us that in the presence of the Eucharist we are indeed in touch with the *mysterium tremendum et fascinans*. The line between the sanctification of the secular and the desecration of the holy is dangerously thin. In Holy Communion the separation between the holy and the common disappears. But the fusion of the two is safe only if, as it were, the thermonuclear reactor is well protected from the surrounding countryside.

I have mentioned in the account that follows how emotionally explosive an issue it proved to try to bring the Eucharist out of the sanctuary and release it from the safe insulation of the ecclesiastical. We have become by now more naturalized to the House Church, but I shall never forget the reaction when first I broached the subject fourteen years ago in a theological college.[3] And what I recall caused most furore was the innocent and incidental remark that if, at this level, 'the chalice and paten become the best "piece" that the household possesses, it may make people realize how unworthy so much modern crockery is of the Lord's table, which is what every Christian table should be'. The thought that there might be contact between the sacred species and cups and saucers was intolerable.

---

[1] Prism Pamphlet, No. 1 (1962), p. 5.
[2] *Ibid.*, p. 2.
[3] In an address 'The House Church and the Parish Church' reprinted in my book *On Being the Church in the World* (1960), pp. 83–95.

But what really brought home to me the passionate and almost pathological resistance to any penetration of the line between the holy and the common was the reaction set off by my remarks at the *Lady Chatterley* trial. In the course of my evidence[1] I quoted William Temple: 'He once said that Christians do not make jokes about sex for the same reason that they do not make jokes about Holy Communion, not because it is sordid, but because it is sacred, and I think Lawrence tried to portray this relation as in a real sense something sacred, as in a real sense an act of holy communion'. I deliberately added after those last two words, for the technical benefit of the press gallery, 'in the lower case', but journalists, like the rest of us, hear what they already understand, and the capital letters in many of the reports have provided fuel for the indignant ever since. But what interests me, more than setting the record right, is the passion that has animated the distortions and misrepresentations. It cannot be explained, I think, simply by the fact that Lawrence (like Shakespeare and Shaw and dozens of others) is describing an adulterous relationship, though that in itself apparently makes it impossible for many to see that he may be saying something important about the sacredness of sex, as distinct from the sanctity of marriage. The vehemence seems to stem from the very association of the act of Holy Communion with the thought of sex as an act of holy communion. That there should be any direct connection between the two—despite all the bridal imagery of Old and New Testaments—breaks down the partition between the sacred and profane (in the sense of that which is 'outside the temple') at too tender a spot. But until this wall is broken down, and the barrier of some of our most deep-seated taboos is pierced, 'liturgy' can never come to 'life'.

(3) I have said in the text that the Eucharist is the most materialistic thing for which the Church comes together. I believe it is now important to add that (of all the things for which it meets 'in church') it is also the least religious. What 'religionless Christianity' may mean for liturgy and worship is something we have hardly begun to understand. I tried to

---

[1] *The Trial of Lady Chatterley*, ed. C. H. Rolph (1961), pp. 70 f.

open up the subject in my section on it in *Honest to God*,[1] but the answers are much more likely to be found by working ministers and laity than by bishops. I am impressed by the evidence of parish priests most alert to the pastoral situation. It seems that people are likely less and less to be drawn to the Church by 'religion'. The traditional pattern presupposes that men and women will be attracted within speaking distance by popular services with popular hymns, at Evensong or People's Services. From that they will graduate (it is hoped) through regular attendance at non-eucharistic religious services to the 'holy of holies' in Communion.

But this pattern is breaking down. In parish after parish in the built-up area of the diocese I serve Matins has disappeared as a public service, and Evensong is probably on the way out. Confirmation candidates are coming forward whose first contact with the worshipping community is at Communion, whether in the parish church or the house church. They respond because they believe that Christ and the Fellowship of the Spirit can provide a clue to the meaning of their lives. But they are secular men, not particularly attracted by religion or interested in joining a religious club. The decisive question is, Can we show them, in Eric James' words,[2] that 'the Eucharist is not primarily a service. It is the meeting of a community'?

To do so will not be easy, particularly at the parish church level. For, as things stand, it *is* primarily a service. Of course, the meeting with the risen Lord in the midst of his people is something that touches every depth and affects every area of human life; and it is entirely proper that it should be given religious expression as it is given musical and artistic expression. By every means, let the liturgy be splendid! But if the music or the decor so dominates that it becomes a concert or a spectacle we recognize the distortion. If the religion dominates so that it becomes a service, it is equally a distortion. But we are slow to recognize it as such. For we have so long identified being a Christian with being religious, in a way that we have never done with being musical. And many people simply are not religious—and in our age they are likely to become

---

[1] 1963, pp. 84–91.   [2] *Op. cit.*, p. 11.

less and less so, if Dietrich Bonhoeffer is correct in his assessment.[1] I believe that Hans Hoekendijk is right in words I have quoted in my essay in *The Honest to God Debate*[2] when he said at Strasbourg in 1960:[3] 'We will not be able really to get alongside man in our modern world unless we begin to "dereligionize" Christianity. Christianity is a secular movement, and this is basic for an understanding of it. We have no business to make it a religion again. That would mean a correction of what Christ has done. And we have no business to make a Christian into a *homo religiosus* again, a religious man, a normal human being plus something. The Christian is simply a man who is in the process of being restored to normal human manhood.'

Liturgy is essentially and primarily a secular activity, as the origin of the word in the sphere of public works testifies. It is concerned (as I try to show) with matter, with society, with action—*ordinary* matter, society and action—*at the level of the holy*, at the level at which it is touched and recreated by the transforming Spirit of Christ. It is not concerned with a special world of its own, but with the making sacred of the secular. But this is not what our services 'say'. They appear to people to be taking them out of this world (even if only to return them to it), instead of bringing this world (in all its secularity) into the power and presence of Christ, as the motion of the Offertory implies. I suspect it is still probably only at the level of the house celebration, at the living-room table or the work-bench, that most people can really *see* that the Communion has to do with the transformation of ordinary things and ordinary relationships. But this is what every celebration should be saying, and our sanctuaries are too religious for secular man to see it. This does not mean they are too holy—often far from it. But it means that the holiness that pervades them is not a worldly holiness: it does not speak to men, in Kierkegaard's phrase, of a 'deeper immersion in existence', of how *their world* can be changed.

I am interested in liturgy only as the clue to the transfiguration of life by the Kingdom of God. And this I believe is the perspective of the New Testament. Let me put it in closing

---

[1] *Letters and Papers from Prison* (1953), beginning with the letter of April 30, 1944.
[2] 1963.
[3] Reproduced in *Student World* LVI (1963), p. 1, in a number devoted to Secularization.

in some words written by the Provost of Southwark:[1] 'The next time Jesus broke bread was not in the next world or in a huge mansion, but round a table after the walk to Emmaus. He was known to them in the breaking of bread. Here is the kingdom. Here is the whole meaning of his coming to consecrate the ordinary, to redeem the secular. In Communion we see ordinary things change; in Communion we see ordinary people made strong; in Communion the Kingdom comes.'

JOHN WOOLWICH

Feast of the Transfiguration, 1963

NOTE

The cover design is taken from the reverse side of my pectoral cross, the obverse bearing the figure of Christ, crucified, between the letters Alpha and Omega. The cross was presented to me by the undergraduates of Clare College and portrays the realities in which our fellowship together was grounded. In the centre stands the ecumenical symbol of the World Council of Churches representing our unity in Christ to-day; underneath it the fish-symbol depicting our link through the ages with the primitive Church; and, on each side, the loaf and the cup we shared at Communion. The chalice was the work of Mr. R. H. Hill, who reproduced it in his own design for the cross.

J.W.

---

[1] E. W. Southcott, *The Parish Comes Alive* (1956), p. 70.

CONTENTS

CONTENTS

I

THE HISTORY AND THEOLOGY
OF AN EXPERIMENT

THE HISTORY AND THEOLOGY
OF AN EXPERIMENT

I. THE SETTING

THIS will be a personal account; but it is not a personal story. It is the story of a group experiment, in which 'we' is always the operative pronoun rather than 'I'. Doubtless I shall have, more frequently than I should wish, to use the word 'I' in the telling of it; for I shall be seeing it through my own eyes, which is the only way I ever saw it and can therefore hope to make it live for others. But the subject of the story is a Christian congregation, and if there is any story worth the telling it is because all that was done was the result of moving forward only on corporate decisions after full discussion and prayer. From which individuals particular ideas came I have now forgotten. And in any case it is irrelevant, since if there proved to be anything in them they were almost certainly not our own. Anything, indeed, that I may have put in I know only too well that I received—and very often lifted quite shamelessly—from others. For liturgy is not 'my line'. And that I suppose would be as good a point as any from which to start.

When I was at my theological college there was no subject that seemed to me so remote from any living concern for the Gospel and its relevance to the modern world than what was taught and examined as 'liturgiology'. And those of my contemporaries who were most enthusiastic about it only confirmed my worst suspicions. For they seemed to be indulging in a purely antiquarian pastime of the narrowest ecclesiastical interest, from which they emerged from time to time to pontificate on what was 'correct' in the public address of the Almighty. This was deduced entirely by precedent and pedigree, and there was no need to stop to ask whether it bore any relation to what the Spirit might be saying to the churches to-day.

The result was that I left my theological college liturgically clueless—which I hasten to add was not its fault, since I had never attended a single lecture in the subject, and contrived to

3

B

get excused it, with a good deal else, from my ordination examination. When I came to do a shortened course after three years' research, it was not among the priorities.

In the parish to which I subsequently went as a curate I was to receive an entirely new vision; for here the Parish Communion formed the centre and power-house of everything that was done in the week, both within the life of the Christian congregation and in the world outside. It was this vision that was decisive, and to it I owe most of such insights as I had to contribute to the experiment I shall be trying to describe. But it was not till some time later, on becoming Dean of Clare College, Cambridge, in 1951, that I found myself responsible for the life of a worshipping community, and thus compelled to think out from an entirely new angle just what was the importance of liturgy and why.

It was then for the first time that I saw the essential connection between liturgy and evangelism, which in practice one had watched going hand-in-hand in the parish. Nothing had originally seemed to me more remote than liturgy from the preaching and presentation of the Gospel. Yet here one was faced with the question, How was the local Church—in this case the Christians in a college of about 400 young men—to become effective as *the witnessing Community*, as the embodiment of the Gospel in action, placarding by its very being and structure the new life by which it lived? As soon as one took seriously the fact that the real instrument of evangelism was the Church, rather than the individual preacher or the isolated Christian, then one found oneself deliberately inviting men to look at the life of the Church, as the Body of Christ and the Fellowship of Holy Spirit, as the place *par excellence* where the Gospel was shown forth. But this meant, above all, inviting them to look, for their vision of the Gospel in action, to the point which, on the Church's own showing, was the focus and power-house—or, in the expressive American idiom, the 'hot-spot'—of its whole existence. Every church of every age has claimed that the Holy Communion, the Mass, the Lord's Supper, constitutes the very centre of its life, the holy of holies of its worship and witness and fellowship. Thus, to direct men's attention to the Church's own life, as the embodiment of the Gospel offer, is above all to direct them to the point in that life from which it all stems, where at the heart of everything the Lord's death is proclaimed till he comes and the powers of the new age are released into this old order of sin, decay and death. It is in the Holy Communion supremely that the Gospel is shown forth: liturgy is the heart of evangelism.

This setting forth of the Gospel is not indeed what the non-Christian will see, nor would he be able to understand it if he did—though St Paul had to insist to the Corinthians that an essential test of their Christian assembly must be the effect it produced on the outsider (1 *Cor.* xiv. 23–5). But even if the outsider is not present at the Liturgy, what is decisive is the conception it conveys to the people of God themselves and the way therefore in which they speak of it. If, as a layman, one really wanted to show men the Gospel in action, the manner by which the kingdoms of this world were being challenged and reduced by the transforming power of God and his Christ, would one immediately point them to the sacrament of Holy Communion as administered in one's own church? Would this be one's working model of the Gospel? That was the question I found myself asking. And I knew that in my own experience the answer was 'no'. In fact, I began to realize with dismay that anyone looking at the typical 'Anglican eight o'clock' of my own tradition might naturally suppose that this was how I understood the Gospel. It was, in fact, about the last embodiment of it to which I should have wished to point them. For there could hardly be anything that would strike them as more individualistic, more pietistic, more unrelated to the stuff and muck of the world where the redemption was meant to be taking place.

These things, I became convinced, ought not to be. It seemed—as it still seems—an intolerable weakness that the Church should be content to live with such a contradiction at the heart of her evangelism. Liturgical reform came to have a priority that a few years before would have seemed to me unthinkable. But it was liturgical reform with a difference. It was not, in the first place, concerned with what I had always imagined liturgical reform to be about—and what, for instance, the 1928 revision of the Prayer Book rite was almost exclusively concerned with—namely, the alteration of what was *said*. It had much more to do with the bringing to adequate expression of what was *done*. And, secondly, it was not liturgical reform for its own sake or in isolation from the rest of the life of the worshipping, witnessing and healing Community. If, in this account, the concentration is upon what we sought to do at the centre, it should be stressed that this was always with a view to what it would enable us to do the more effectively at the circumference.

It was with this growing conviction of the centrality of liturgy to evangelism that I found myself asking how in Clare we might become more deeply aware of what it meant for us to *be* the Church (in distinction from merely 'going to Chapel'), first at the heart of our worship and then right through the life of the College. The Chapel, I recall stressing in my first Chapel Letter, was not simply a building to go to. Its true conception was to be seen rather in the use of the same term for the local branch of certain trades unions. The Christians in the College were, as it were, the local branch of Christ's union, set there, simply in virtue of their baptism, to be 'his men' in the place.

This conception of 'the Church in the College', transcending any sectional loyalties, is one that came to be implicit in everything we sought to do and to be. In some other Cambridge colleges it subsequently became quite explicit, and besides the Chapel Card, which goes out to every member, there was another belonging to 'the Church in the College' which was put up only by those who thus indicated their Christian profession and accepted the responsibilities of it. I am inclined to think that this draws the line too sharply and self-consciously in a society where the great majority of its members are baptized and confirmed. One had always to strike a balance between insisting on 'the gathered Church', the committed congregation, as the instrument of any effective action, and insisting also that the whole College by its very title was a 'religious foundation', a Christian society, which publicly, and, indeed, at considerable expense, maintained its witness to the Christian Faith. But though the conception of the Church in the College may have been implicit rather than explicit, it was, none the less, fundamental. The whole basis of what we sought to do was that every Christian in the College, whatever tradition or denomination he might belong to, whatever other religious organization he might or might not join, was before anything else a member of the Church of God as it found its local expression in Clare. The Chapel, while he was there, was his parish Church.

The corollary of this is that the Chapel is the parish Church of every member of the College and must seek to be so as far as this is possible. This presents it with a unique ecumenical responsibility and opportunity. The ancient Cambridge and Oxford colleges are Anglican foundations. This means in the first place that their Chapels should aim to be the spiritual home of all members of the Church of England for the time being within their walls—and these will be as diverse as the Church of England is comprehensive. This demands, I believe, that the Chapel should be faithful to the ideal of 'the complete Church of England man', abjuring party extremism (and at the same time any watery *via media*), stressing the things that unite rather than the things that divide. In these days, when the traditional party lines are becoming yearly more obsolete, this is not anything like as difficult as it used to be. The 'catholic'-'evangelical' split is not, I believe, a live issue in Cambridge to-day—though it appears that in Oxford things are still very different—except where it is deliberately kept alive. The newer type of high churchmanship, which has emerged from the revival of biblical theology and the liturgical movement, and which really is concerned with a high doctrine of the Church as the Body of Christ, is one that is equally at home in 'evangelical' as in 'catholic' circles. Certainly, the way we were led to do things in Clare, which its worst enemies could not describe as a mere compromise, was one that made party issues singularly irrelevant, and which no serious body of Christian opinion desired to see otherwise. I sometimes took a quiet delight in observing how features in our 'use', inspired as they had been for the most part by the more liturgically-minded parishes (which meant usually the more 'high church' parishes) and even by the liturgical movement in the Church of Rome, in fact, commended themselves most immediately to the evangelicals, and often very conservative evangelicals, while the anglo-catholics, at the beginning, were a good deal more suspicious.

But the challenge presented to the worship of a college chapel is much greater than that of providing a unifying churchmanship for all the members of the Church of England. The College community is a cross-section, religiously, of the country (though it is still true of Cambridge that the dominance of the public school entry means an untypically large percentage of Anglicans, and of confirmed Anglicans). The Chapel, therefore, must, if it is not to become merely sectional and sectarian, set itself to be the Chapel of the College and not merely of the church-going Anglicans. The Roman Catholics and Free Churchmen have, of course, churches and chaplaincies in the city, as do the Anglicans, with which they have every duty to link themselves. But the College, unless it is to degenerate into a mere hostel, is the community to which they 'belong'; and it would be a sad day for the health of that community if that ceased to be true of the spiritual, as of every other, level of its common life. The Roman Catholics will, of course, always go their own way, although, outside the Chapel building, there are Christian concerns on which from time to time they can be drawn in. But the Free Churchmen must be made to feel that it is also their Chapel. Its liturgy and its clergy, indeed, are Anglican, but I am convinced from experience that it is possible to go a very long way towards integrating them in a genuinely ecumenical community, alike in worship and in witness.

At this point the decisive factor, I am sure, is the freedom, regularized by the Upper Houses of the Convocations of Canterbury and York in January 1933, by which full communicants of any Christian denomination may, as members of the College community, be admitted to Communion in the College Chapel.[1] This freedom, I am persuaded, should be used to the full. It provides a unique opportunity of building up, round the Prayer Book liturgy, a genuinely ecumenical community, such, indeed, as the Anglican Settlement originally

---

[1] Attempts have been made to undermine this freedom. It is true that the resolutions were passed only by the Upper Houses. Although the Lower Houses considered the resolutions, they were not asked to approve them: for their object was to give general guidance to *the bishops* in the exercise of their pastoral discretion in admitting non-Anglicans to Communion under various circumstances. The clause about school and college chapels proved entirely non-controversial and was, in fact, alluded to only once in the debate in either Convocation, when Archbishop Lang of Canterbury, in summing up, said that it merely gave official recognition to long-established practice with which there was no desire to interfere.

It is true also that the freedom is given, according to the Canterbury resolution, in the singular, for the admission to Communion of 'a member of the Society who, being baptized, has the status of a communicant in his own denomination'. But since it applies to *any* member who fulfils this condition, it is a mere quibble to say that it precludes (as has been urged) a general invitation to *all* such members. In the York resolution the wording is, in fact, in the plural.

envisaged. Experience has shown that the Prayer Book service, if used with intelligence and imagination, presents no insuperable barrier to this—though something like the Liturgy of the Church of South India would certainly have been a more adequate vehicle of expression than the 1662 rite, and that not only for the sake of the non-Anglicans. But of one thing I am convinced, and that is that at present the Book of Common Prayer provides the only operative focus of unity. Depart from it in any serious way, and the sole basis for Anglican unity has gone, let alone for anything wider. In the form of service used at Clare, the order was more strictly that of the Prayer Book than in many churches that would claim to be most traditionally Anglican. Our concern was with letting the action speak rather than with changing what was said. Of course, the latter *is* of great importance, and reform of the 1662 rite must in due course come. But first let us make sure we know what we are *doing*, and then let the words give it the most articulate and splendid expression of which we and the past are capable. Moreover, the road to living liturgical reform leads from the bottom upwards, and that is why controlled experiment in the local worshipping community, especially at the sub-parochial or house church level, is so vital to the health of the Body of Christ. Nothing lasting will be achieved, as 1928 showed, by imposition from the top downwards.

But this is a diversion from my present point, which is that for the first time for four hundred years Christians in England are beginning to speak a common eucharistic language. This was brought home to us most vividly when we came after some years of experiment to attempt to articulate what we were doing and communicate it to those coming newly into it—a most essential task in a parish where a third of the congregation changed each year, and one which we found considerably easier than we dared to hope. We decided to try to produce our own Communion manual, which should both set out and explain the service as we actually did it and enable individuals to enter devotionally into it. No one who knows anything of this genre of literature[1] is likely to underestimate the difficulty

[1] Since our own manual was produced in 1954, a number of others on the same lines have appeared both for local and general use. Among the latter are *The Communion Service* (ed. M. Stockwood; S.C.M. Press, 1s. 6d.) and *At Parish Communion* (ed. E. O. Sheilds; Mowbrays, 1s. 6d.).

of such a project. In the first place, it required the creation, it is hardly too much to say, of a new devotional theology. The theology underlying the traditional Communion manuals both 'catholic' and 'evangelical' has been incorrigibly individualistic, pietistic and subjective. In England, at any rate, the liturgical movement has so far produced no body of devotional material that really enables the individual to 'pray into' the Liturgy as it has come to be transformed in outward practice—a point, I believe, of real weakness in the revival. Moreover, the very fact that Communion manuals have until recently had to be classified as 'catholic' and 'evangelical' indicates that there has been no common language even within the Church of England. Sometimes, indeed, as one picks up these little books, the divergence of idiom seems so wide that one is not surprised that the comprehensiveness of the English Church has proved something of a *stupor mundi*. Finally, almost all Communion manuals betray the marks of having been composed *by* the clergy (who by definition have not the opportunity to use them) *for* the laity—as witness the tell-tale 'you' of instruction that runs through them ('you may now sit', or 'say this to yourself').

We determined that ours should really be produced by the people for the people—the whole people of God who were going to use it. Moreover, if it was to serve those for whom it was intended, it was imperative that it should genuinely represent the corporate understanding of the Eucharist which we had come to share. It was, indeed, a test of whether this corporate understanding could bear articulation. But by making sure that every part of every draft was thoroughly revised in small groups which were representative of all shades of opinion, Anglican and non-Anglican, we hammered out something which I believe was a revelation to us all of what has now become possible. No doubt every individual among us would have preferred something in it to be different. (A Methodist ordinand, I remember, was very anxious to expunge all reference to the fact that the wine was real wine from the cellar!) Nevertheless, we had found a language, not only of theological explanation, but of devotion in which we all could share. And we found it mainly by a return to the Bible and the early liturgies, whose theology of the Body of Christ in relation both to the Church and the Sacrament, antedates the mediaeval divisions and distortions to which we all are heirs. The result, for what it is worth, is printed as the last section of this book.[1]

This was but one example of the enrichment that came to our life and witness from the integration at every level of the non-Anglican element in our College Communion. I stress the words 'at every level' because the laity of all traditions were prepared to enter unreservedly into the action, taking such share in it as in other circumstances might have been reserved for a special class of 'servers'. For a time, too, we were able to use a Presbyterian minister in residence as a research student to assist with the administration of the chalice, regarding it as a legitimate extension, within such an ecumenical community, to allow to a non-Anglican minister what in principle any layman can do and which is now being widely permitted to lay-readers. On one occasion—during the week of prayer for Christian unity—we were able to give the other cup to a former member of the College who had recently been ordained to the Methodist ministry; and I remember as my eye caught him administering in turn to an Anglo-Catholic, a Baptist and a Quaker, wondering if there was anywhere else where this could happen! Indeed, if we had had a sufficient proportion of Free Churchmen to justify it (and Clare must have had one of the lowest in the University), I have seriously thought that the appointment of a Free Church chaplain would be the proper complement to the Anglican Dean, and that they should concelebrate at the Table together.[2]

I have spoken of some of the implications of the Church being the Church in such a catholic community, in the widest sense of that word, as a Cambridge College. I have insisted that liturgy, true and relevant worship, lies at the very heart of its evangelistic task, and that the Holy Communion is the creative centre of the whole life of the people of God. For it is here by partaking of Christ's Body, becoming bone of his bone and flesh of his flesh, that we 'become what we are', his

[1] Separate copies are obtainable from The Dean, Clare College, Cambridge, at 2s. 8d., post free.

[2] For the important but neglected possibilities of concelebration in an ecumenical context I would refer to my articles 'Intercommunion and Concelebration' and 'Episcopacy and Intercommunion' reprinted in my book On Being the Church in the World (S.C.M. Press, 1960).

Body in the world. How then did we set about turning these convictions into reality?

First, let me say, as I should have said before, that much to which I have been referring was indeed a reality well before I came on the scene. I can but take up the story, in any personal way, where I came in. But no one could have been more blessed in his predecessors, one of whom remained as a constant colleague, inspiration and friend. They must not be held responsible for the account that I am giving (and that is another reason why 'I' must constantly alternate with 'we'); but without the foundation they laid, pastorally and theologically, nothing would have been possible. It was not only that I came into what was by every external mark a 'going concern', a united Chapel-going community from whose worship no section of Christians in the College (except, of course, the Roman Catholics) stood aloof. I also found ready-made many of the channels that were later to prove so invaluable. Full use was already made of the permission to welcome non-Anglicans to Communion; there had for years been a regular Communion breakfast on Sundays, which had only to be transferred from the Dean's room to the small Dining Hall when it burst at the seams; the Chapel Meeting, which was extended to become the instrument of all decisions and policy, was already a lively example of Christian democracy; the termly Open Meeting, which proved our main opportunity for 'frontier' evangelism, was an established institution; and Clare was the only College, and until recently remained so, which regularly sent out with its Chapel Card a Chapel Letter, which formed an indispensable instrument for putting it all over.

Add to this the fact that I arrived in a boom period in Cambridge religion, when the College Chapels had never been fuller,[1] into one of the most friendly and united Colleges in the University, with a Governing Body which allowed us an almost entirely free hand, with a compact congregation of as lively and intelligent young men as could be found in the country, with no money to be raised and two ordained colleagues—and it begins to sound like the parson's dream parish. There were, of course, things to be set on the other

---

[1] Numbers, in fact, in College Chapels continued to rise all the time I was in Cambridge. In my eight years at Clare our average number of communicants doubled, the highest number in my first term being exactly the same as the lowest in my last.

side. A College community is an artificial parish, with no women or children except those of dons and staff; it is there at all only in short and highly concentrated bursts, which from a liturgical point of view take the heart out of the Christian Year, leaving one without Christmas, Holy Week or Easter; it is a highly mobile congregation, most of whom pass on after three years; and the Church in Cambridge is very properly up against some of the best opposition in the world. But it would be ungracious not to confess from the beginning that the conditions were about as favourable as they could be.

Indeed, it is because of this, and because of the quite disproportionate share of her ministerial manpower that the Church, quite rightly, allots[1] to a strategic centre like Cambridge, that a special responsibility rests with such communities to be a source of creative experiment for the Church as a whole. Moreover, the considerable ecclesiastical freedom which historically they have enjoyed lays an obligation upon them to use that freedom both creatively and responsibly. The College Chapel is under no bishop or vicar—indeed, in Clare we were in the doubly 'peculiar' position of being extra-parochial in a parish which was itself extra-diocesan. The Governing Body is its own ordinary, or ecclesiastical authority, and I was in the position of being one-thirtieth part of the ordinary—a nice example of pure Presbyterian polity at the heart of an Anglican foundation: I represented, as it were, the preaching elder. It would have been an easy freedom to abuse, though, indeed, there was sometimes not so much real freedom as there sounds. From time to time one wished for a bishop to whom one could have gone and said: 'Is this, spiritually speaking, a good and legitimate experiment?' Decisions of this kind one had, after consultation, to take on

[1] 'Allots' perhaps is hardly the right word. None of the College clergy are there because of any ecclesiastical policy or direction, nor does a penny of their stipends come from Church funds. It is a signal example of great secular institutions (albeit in this case religious foundations) creating openings for the Church because, on the whole, the Church has justified their confidence. This is particularly true of the modern Cambridge College Chaplains. (No such system exists at Oxford, which is the single most important reason for the difference in the state of health of the College Chapels in the two places.) The Chaplain at a Cambridge College, in distinction from the Dean, is normally not a Fellow with academic responsibilities. He is appointed solely on his pastoral qualifications and for that task. Materially speaking, the College appears at first sight to get little or no return for its money, and it is a tribute to what the Chaplains have made of the job, particularly since the last war, that it is becoming more and more unthinkable that a College should not now make such an appointment.

one's own. For the only sort of question which a Governing Body as such is likely to be able to answer is: 'Is this legal according to the College Statutes (which in our case were so vaguely phrased as not even to require Christian services!) or the University Tests Act of 1871?'

But the real issues that the freedom posed were not legal. They were bound up with such questions as, 'How far ahead of the main body of Church opinion ought one to go?', or, 'How could one give men a vision of something beyond what they had been used to and at the same time fit them to go out into the main stream of parochial life with something relevant to give?' This need for being in vital touch with the parishes, and for training in lay responsibility within the life of a parish, formed, indeed, one of our constant themes in vacation visits, sermon courses and group discussions. For a College is for most of its inmates only a transit camp, and must not foster a kind of religion or churchmanship that is applicable and viable solely within its own abnormal and privileged situation. Nevertheless, it is in the situation where we are that we must always learn to be the Church, and it is in these conditions that we sought to incarnate any vision we were given.

2. ACTION

I have already said that our liturgical concern had more to do with what was done than with what was said. This is because liturgy is at its heart social action. The very term 'liturgy' derives from two Greek words, *laos* and *ergon*, meaning 'people' and 'work'. Liturgy is public work—and, indeed, in its original secular context 'public works'. It is the *ergon*, the action, of the *laos*, or people of God. And the command of Jesus laying the celebration of the Eucharist upon the Church was expressed in the simplest possible charge: '*Do this*'—and the verb is in the plural. The significance of the plural, the fact that this is essentially *social* action, will be the theme of the next section. But first we must pause on the fact that it is action.

To the ordinary way of thinking the Holy Communion is a 'service' (as in the familiar phrase 'the early service'), and for the most part it consists of words—words used by the minister, or words used together, words said or words sung. It is, to be sure, the only service during which all the people—and not only the minister—have to move from their seats. At one point they have to 'go up', and this breaks the otherwise continuous sequence of words and silences. But the structure thus interrupted is essentially a pattern of prayers, readings and more prayers, with perhaps hymns and a sermon for intermission. The focus of it all is, indeed, a moment of intense silence, but this would more naturally be described in terms of inaction rather than action, or if in terms of activity, then of personal spirituality rather than of public works.

It has been the contribution of the late Dom Gregory Dix to bring home to our generation the fact that 'the shape of the liturgy', to use the title of his great work, is constructed not round any pattern of words, like Mattins or Evensong, but round the four-fold *action* of Jesus at the Last Supper. I shall ever be grateful that the reading of this book was postponed for me, for reasons I have already indicated, till I was driven to it by the exigencies of a pastoral situation. Even though Dix may need to be watched at every point, there can be no doubt that *The Shape of the Liturgy* will live, not only as a superb piece of English prose,[1] but as a masterly presentation (which any intelligent layman can follow through its 750 pages) of what the living organism of the Liturgy has been and is. I read it at the beginning of my time in Clare, and those who know it will see how much it has moulded what follows—in particular the course of addresses on the meaning of the Eucharist that were first sketched out under its impact.

The action of Jesus at the Last Supper when he took, and blessed, and broke, and gave, is what ever since has shaped the structure of the Eucharist. But this action was itself in the first instance but the acting out, for the disciples' comprehension and subsequent participation, of what Jesus was about to *do*, in the 'finished act' of Good Friday and Easter. And it is to this decisive act that the Eucharist goes back. It is not a memorial of the Last Supper—though the Last Supper determines its form as a common meal. It is a memorial of the Lord's death

---

[1] As specimens for any anthology, I would cite the paragraph on p. 395 which begins: 'There is a sort of pause in events round about the turn of the century'; or the paragraph on p. 744 beginning: 'Was ever another command so obeyed?', painting so vividly and movingly the variety of circumstance and style in which men throughout the ages have 'done this'.

and resurrection, till he comes. What it makes contemporary for us is not the events of the Upper Room, but the events of Golgotha and Easter Day. The Eucharist is *the* Christian action, the heart of all Christian action in the world, because it mediates and makes present, in all its efficacy and power, the great saving act of God in Christ once and for all wrought out on Calvary. For all Christian action in this world is really nothing else than the finished work of Christ becoming operative through his body, the Church. And the Eucharist is *the* point where that finished work is constantly renewed to the Church, as those who have already been buried and raised with Christ in Baptism come to share in the broken body and outpoured blood of him whose crucified and life-giving body they are called to be. This is the point where all Christian action begins, where we are united with his act, and where what he has done *for* us is renewed *within* us for transmission to the world. This is the crucible of the new creation, in which God's new world is continually being fashioned out of the old, as ordinary men and women are renewed and sent out as the carriers of Christ's risen life.

Now if the Eucharist is thus the heart and hub of social action, the point where this world is taken and consecrated, broken and restored for God and his kingdom, and where the Church itself is renewed as the agent of the Christian revolution, then we must learn again what the early Church meant when it spoke so naturally of 'doing the Eucharist'. (Contrast the modern phrases, 'saying' or 'hearing' Mass, 'going to' Communion, etc. The nearest equivalent, '*making* my Communion', shows how far we have moved.) Here, as so often in our thinking at Clare, we found ourselves going back to the theology and practice of the Church of the early centuries. And it is as well to say at once that this sprang from no antiquarian concern or romantic revival, such as is conjured up, for instance, in the unhappy title given to the film-strip of an earlier experiment[1] from which we learnt much: 'Towards a Patristic Ceremonial'. If we found inspiration and at points a model for action in the way things were 'done' in the pre-Nicene Church, it was because their theology was whole and sound, not because of any desire to return to an imaginary golden age, or to write off developments since. Indeed, one

---

[1] At the Queen's College, Birmingham.

of the most recent liturgies of any church, that of the Church of South India, is, as I said, in many ways the best theological expression of what we were aiming to bring out—and that because it is grounded in the same theology of the Eucharist and its relation to the action of the Church.

When we come together to 'do' the Eucharist, it is to set forth and set forward the action of God in Christ for the redemption and renewal of this world order. We come, first, to proclaim the mighty acts of God, to 'celebrate and set forth' what Christ has done *for* us. For this, for sheer exultant thanksgiving and celebration, the Prayer Book liturgy is, indeed, seriously inadequate, focusing attention solely on Calvary and its propitiation for sin. But whatever its limitations, we must do everything we can, in Abbé Michonneau's words, to 'let the liturgy be splendid'. This does not mean making it elaborate or heavily ritualistic—that depends entirely on the style appropriate to the level at which it is being celebrated: a meal will be very different round the kitchen table and at the Lord Mayor's Banquet. In the severity of a classical eighteenth-century Chapel we in fact abjured almost all flourish. An example of this was our very restricted use of music. We always had hymns, which can add greatly to 'the song of them that triumph, the shout of them that feast'. At first I believed that we should also be led to singing other parts of the service, particularly the *Sanctus* and the *Gloria in Excelsis*, and we did, indeed, have sung celebrations on special occasions. But they never really 'went'. Whereas to hear seventy-five or a hundred young men standing and shouting— well, perhaps that *is* an exaggeration!—the *Sursum Corda* and the *Gloria* convinced me that for us, at any rate, this was the medium of proclamation.

Nor must one minimize or obscure the proclamation that is made through the Liturgy of the Word. Indeed, one of the things to which we gave greatest thought is how this could be rescued from the merely preliminary and subordinate position of 'ante-communion' which it has come to occupy in Anglican usage. The *synaxis* or Liturgy of the Word is in structure and origin independent of the Eucharist. It has its own pattern, which is not that of action but of word, and its own centre, which is not the communion table but the lecterns from which the Scriptures are read and expounded. In order to bring this

out, we took this part of the service not from the sanctuary
(to which the ministers moved only at the Offertory) but from
the body of the Chapel. Moreover, just as in the second half
of the service the prime purpose is to let the Action speak, so
here it is to let the Word speak. This means that it must be
expounded and made contemporary, as the Prayer Book rubric
specifically requires, in preaching; and a sermon I believe to
be an indispensable instrument for the regular communication
of any thorough-going theology of the Eucharist and its
implications. Certainly it was through the term's course of
sermons at the College Communion—reproduced, in revised
form, later in this book—that almost all the changes we made
were originally set in motion.

But the Scriptures themselves must also be allowed to speak,
and great importance attaches, I believe, not only to the way
they are read (and a layman always read the Epistle and one
of the deacons the Gospel), but to the version in which they
are read. In Free Church worship the tendency is for the
vehicle of worship, the prayers, to be in contemporary speech,
while the lessons remain in sonorous archaism of the Authorized Version. This I believe to be almost exactly the wrong
way round. Let the liturgical forms, as long as they are
intelligible, ring with echoes of the Church's worship down
the centuries, but let the Word of God be contemporary,
speaking to every man in his own language, cutting through
all that muffles and stifles its impact. When the new official
translation of the Bible is published, one hopes that it will be
immediately commended for liturgical use, though, since the
Epistles and Gospels are incorporated in the Act of Uniformity
(and are therefore the only part of the so-called Authorized
Version to be authorized!), it will need special vigilance to see
that the Communion service is not expressly excluded—
particularly as many will instinctively feel that this is much
too 'holy' for modern idiomatic English, however good. But
this false sense of holiness (of which more in due course),
which bedevils the attitude, especially of the laity, to the Holy
Communion at almost every point, must somehow be broken
through. In the meanwhile, we found that reading the
Epistle, at least, from J. B. Phillips' version blew away some
of the cobwebs, and also some sleep from the eyes at eight
o'clock in the morning.

But we must return to the action of the Eucharist proper. In the first place, as I have said, this action commemorates and sets forth what God in Christ has done *for* us. But it also sets forward the redemptive work of Christ *in* us, enabling us as the Body of Christ to become what by his act he has made us. The action by which Christ spelt out to the disciples the meaning of his sacrifice, showing them how his life was to be taken and consecrated, broken and poured out for the world, are the same actions that he lays upon us. 'This do ye.' As in Baptism, the pattern of Christ's obedience has to be made ours, and not only decisively once and for all but continuously, if we are really to 'be in him and he in us'. The way in which the four actions, done with the bread and wine of our lives, of Taking, Blessing, Breaking and Sharing, hammer home this pattern is brought out sufficiently in the sermons and the manual that follow, and need not be expanded here. But somehow we must let the actions stand forth from the words which are meant to clothe them. That is, indeed, not easy in the 1662 Liturgy, where the Offertory has been separated from the Thanksgiving or Blessing, and the Fraction been absorbed into the Prayer of Consecration. But, pending revision, we must do our best, and that is what we attempted to do. The manner in which we did it is bound up with the spreading of the action through the congregation as a whole and is best described under the next heading of Society.

But before we leave the subject of Action, something further of great importance remains to be said. We come to the Eucharist not merely to celebrate and set forth what Christ has done *for* us, not merely to set forward and perfect his redemption *in* us by the union of our lives with his, but to offer ourselves as the instruments of his action *through* us. The pattern of action to which we have yielded ourselves in the Eucharist is the pattern of all Christian action, as the redemption wrought by Christ is taken out into the lives and relationships of men by those who constitute his Body. If the Liturgical Movement does nothing more than affect how things are 'done' in Church, then it will not escape the judgement that fell on the Oxford Movement, especially in some of its later forms, where an introspective interest in the Church replaced a concern for the Kingdom, that is, for God's action in the world. The Eucharist is, indeed, bound up with the

Church, the Body of Christ, from beginning to end. But at its institution (*St Mark* xiv. 25; *St Luke* xxii. 15-18) Jesus related it specifically to the coming of the Kingdom. For it is here that we taste the powers of the age to come, and eat the bread and drink the cup new with Christ in his kingdom. Yet attaching to the whole rite is what Karl Barth has called an 'awful preliminariness': every celebration points forward to the day 'when sacraments shall cease', when the bread and wine of this world shall be 'fulfilled in the kingdom of God'. And that does not only point us away to the moment of final *Parousia*, 'till he comes'; it points us out to the kingship of Christ as yet unacknowledged in our midst. The Eucharist, as *the* Christian action from which all other Christian action flows, is the most political act to which the Church sets its hand. As we expressed it at the end of our Communion Manual, 'The sharing of Bread, concluded now sacramentally, must be continued socially—and thence economically and politically'. The implications of this we shall consider under the third heading of Matter; but we leave the discussion of Action with the reminder again that Liturgy belongs to the sphere of public works—and that for the Christian is an essentially *spiritual* activity, begun at the altar, the workshop of the new world, but continued at the bench, started at what the Prayer Book so splendidly describes as 'God's board' but finished at ours.

3. SOCIETY

From the beginning I have stressed that the action of the Liturgy is social action. In the most important sense, of course, it is Christ's action. He is the doer, the breaker of bread, or it is nothing. But it is never Christ's action in isolation, but the action of the *Totus Christus*, of Christ in his Body. The celebrant of the Eucharist is Christ, but it is also the Church. What it is not is what our usage continually asserts that it is, namely, the priest or minister. The presbyter or bishop was never called 'the celebrant' in the primitive Church, but 'the president'. And in that distinction there is a world of difference. It is the difference between the two worlds of the early Church and the mediaeval Church, between the conception of the

Eucharist as a celebration of the whole Body of Christ and the conception of the Eucharist as something done *by* the priest *for* the people. And, as Dix showed in his earlier and fascinating account in the volume of essays entitled *The Parish Communion*,[1] this mediaeval development has been with us all, Catholic and Protestant, ever since. In practice, if not in theory, most of what the Reformers achieved was that, whereas previously the priest's duty was to say Mass for the people, it was now his function to provide Communion for the people.

And from this derives the notion which (together with the false sense of holiness already mentioned) is in my experience the single greatest psychological barrier to a true understanding of the Eucharist. It is the idea that the priest is there to 'put on' a celebration each week (or more frequently, or less, according to what passes for 'churchmanship'), to which the faithful can 'go', as it were, to fill up, as their sense of piety or duty or need dictates. Whether or how often they go is a private matter between the individual and God; and the congregation on any given Sunday, like the customers at a filling station, will be simply those of the regulars (with a scattering of visitors and occasionals) who desire that week to avail themselves of the Church's ministrations. The conception is so familiar to us that it need not be described further. It is, I suspect, that upon which virtually every one of us was brought up and from which we find it almost impossible to free ourselves. Even those clergy who have come to be convinced that weekly Communion is the ideal so often present this (or are understood by their people to present this) simply as a 'stepping up' of the existing pattern. The call seems to be just one more clerical appeal, made so insistently at the time of the Oxford Movement but heard equally at the Reformation and, indeed, throughout Church history, for more frequent Communion. It is not this at all. Indeed, the effect of the Liturgical Movement is likely to be in the direction of reducing rather than of multiplying Masses. But how to get the difference across is something I have never felt I have succeeded in doing, and shall doubtless not succeed in doing now.

[1] Ed. A. G. Hebert (S.P.C.K., 1937), pp. 97-143.

It is not that the picture I have described is simply wrong—
that would be to condemn whole generations of God's
children. It is its sole sufficiency which makes it look so
inadequate when it is set against the other picture that pre-
vailed in the Church of the apostolic and subsequent ages.
There is an entire dimension of Christian understanding which
it leaves out, namely, that we come to Communion not
merely to feed upon the Body of Christ, but to be created the
Body of Christ. That we come, as individuals, to receive 'the
spiritual food of the most precious Body and Blood of our
Saviour Jesus Christ' is something for which all our Confirmation teaching has prepared us; that we come as the local
Church, thereby to be renewed and sent out as his Body in
the world, is something which remains psychologically alien.
And, indeed, the Prayer Book hardly helps us. The Catechism
defines 'the benefits' of the Lord's Supper simply as 'the
strengthening and refreshing of our souls by the Body and
Blood of Christ, as our bodies are by the Bread and Wine',
and the Order for Holy Communion contains but a single
reference (in the Prayer of Thanksgiving) to the fundamental
Pauline conception of the Body of Christ as 'the blessed
company of all faithful people'.

But once we begin to grasp that it is essentially as the
Church, and individually as members of it, that we come, that
Communion is not something that 'I' can 'make' but only 'we'
can 'do', then the picture begins to look very different. When
St Paul introduced his remarks with the words, 'When you
come together', he did not need to specify further that he was
going on to speak of the Eucharist; for this was *the* thing,
indeed, the only thing, for which it was quite essential for the
Church to 'come together'. This was the gathering for which
the Lord's Day existed, and by which alone it was for hundreds
of years distinguished from any other working day. To be a
member of the Body and not to be *there* was *ipso facto* to be a
sick member of the Body, whether physically or spiritually.
Not to take one's place at the family table was necessarily to
side with the world. This was no 'early service' one went to
if one was specially pious: it *was* the Church being the Church,[1]

[1] Cf. the equivalence of 'When you come together' (1 Cor. xi. 17), 'When you
assemble as a church' (xi. 18), and 'When you meet together, it is not the Lord's
supper that you eat' (xi. 20).

as Sunday by Sunday it met with its risen Lord to be recreated and built up as his body in the world. It is, indeed, '*because* there is one loaf, as St Paul said, that 'we who are many are' one body; for we all partake of the same loaf' (1 *Cor*. x. 17: Revised Standard Version).[1]

The one loaf, the symbol and the source of our unity with our Head and with his members, is something that stands in urgent need of recovery both in our theology and practice. With the common cup, never mercifully lost in Anglicanism (as it has been denied in Romanism and dissipated in Protestantism), the single loaf is so potent a symbol that only a theology that had become grievously individualistic could have substituted for it separate wafers or 'breads' (the very plural is unknown elsewhere). It is also, as we discovered, only with a common loaf, which really needs to be broken for distribution, that the *Fraction* truly comes to its own, with its important symbolism that the life of God can be given and shared, only if it is broken and poured out. The Fraction in the Prayer Book rite has become a purely residual act, performed symbolically by the priest as he mimes the action of Jesus at the Last Supper in the course of the Prayer of Consecration.[2] It has ceased altogether to be one of the four actions of the service itself, from which, indeed, its earliest name, the Breaking of the Bread, derived. Our own practice at Clare was to obey the Prayer Book instruction by which the priest breaks the loaf, symbolically, as he recites the words of institution, but then to let what one might call the business part of the Fraction be taken up as a separate act by the deacons.[3] In the same way, the priest began the administration by communicating those at the Table, and then, if there were sufficient of them, committed to those functioning as deacons their proper task of ministering to the people.

---

[1] This is a key Pauline text, of decisive importance for the constitutive relation of the Eucharist to the Church, and it is one of the calamities of translation that the Authorized Version failed to bring out the causal relationship between the two, rendering (scarcely intelligibly): 'For we being many are one bread, and one body.'

[2] For the baleful development of this *vide* E. L. Mascall, *Corpus Christi*, ch. 3 (Longmans, Green & Co., 1953).

[3] Where a fraction was necessary for distribution, as it would have been with the use of common bread during the seventeenth and eighteenth centuries, it undoubtedly continued to occupy its traditional position before the Communion. No rubric was necessary to cover what would automatically have been done. In the Scottish Prayer Book the priest is, in fact, instructed to break the bread *twice*, once in the Prayer of Consecration and again before Communion.

This last point introduces a principle upon which we came to lay some stress in our concern to recover the understanding of the Eucharist as the action of the whole Body of Christ. Another way of describing what happened with the beginning of the Middle Ages is to speak of the clericalization of the Eucharist. A combination of bad theology and illiteracy led to the concentration of the whole service in the hands of the priest, as the only person who did or said or read anything. In the early Church the bishop or priest was (as has been said) not the celebrant but the president, whose special liturgy in and on behalf of the whole Body was to offer the prayer of blessing over the bread and the wine and to break the bread. This, originally the *only* prayer in the Eucharistic action proper, was that for which, liturgically speaking, he was ordained and set apart. But the rest of the action was not peculiarly his. In fact, again in and on behalf of the whole Body, it was performed by those to whom each part properly belonged—deacons, readers, prophets, and the rest. And the whole action could not begin at all without the Offertory, which was, and is, the peculiar liturgy of the laity—a theological principle of considerable significance to which we shall return.

Any attempt to recover this corporate structure within the confines of the Prayer Book liturgy must again be limited. But once more we tried to do what we could, stripping from the presiding priest those parts of the Liturgy that do not essentially belong to him, and stressing and extending what the whole congregation says and does *together*. The details of all this are sufficiently indicated in the Manual and its rubrics. (Fortunately rubrics, though in many ways the most important part of liturgy, as they regulate the things done, are not regarded by the ordinary Englishman as nearly so sacrosanct as words, and a good deal of adjustment to circumstance can be made without what I came to call the 'Prayer Book fundamentalists' really noticing!) But two points call for a little elaboration—the part of the deacons and the role of the laity.

Deacons played an important part in the primitive liturgy (if only, as Hippolytus indicates, as 'chuckers-out'!). Indeed, theirs was primarily a *liturgical* office. (Contrary to popular impression, 'the seven' of *Acts* vi. 1-6 are never called 'deacons', and they were certainly not the same as the 'deacons' referred to in *Philippians* i. 1 and the Pastoral Epistles in close conjunction with 'bishops', whose ministrants they were.) Their function, as their name indicates, was that of 'servers', though this involved much more, including the actual administration (*the diakonia*, or deaconing), than that pale and attenuated office to-day. The diaconate, too, in modern Church order has become a mere probationary office for the priesthood. But every priest, and bishop, is in deacon's orders, and it is good that he should be reminded of this. When we had a man, for instance, among the research students, who was only ordained deacon we naturally employed him in his proper function. But usually the deacons' part was taken by those who were also priests, though since they were acting in their capacity as deacons they wore their stoles deacon-wise, across the shoulder.

Ideally, where there are several priests in a local congregation, they should each be exercising the highest function in the Liturgy for which they are ordained, and should concelebrate at the Table together. But this presupposes, as in the early Church, that there are other orders in the Body, each of which is also exercising its proper function in the total concelebration of the people of God. In our modern situation the effect, I was convinced,[1] would merely be to *widen* the gulf between the clergy and the laity, and to give the impression that the whole action was concentrated in the hands of a clerical club. For this reason we made as much as possible of the deacons as the link between the presiding priest and the people. It was they who received the offertory, performed all the preparation and ablutions, announced the hymns and notices, led the confession, broke the loaf, administered the bread and wine, and one of them was responsible, earlier, for reading the Gospel, to which the Ordinal specifically commissions them.

All this is complementary, too, to the proper part of the laity. It is ironical that the only active part in the Liturgy we have given to the laity, that of 'serving', is one that does not properly belong to them. Quite apart from its historical association with the diaconate, it is for the most part a fairly technical job, which involves a certain amount of training and esoteric know-how that limits it in practice to a particular class

[1] But cf. B. Minchin, *Every Man in his Ministry* (Darton, Longman and Todd, 1960).

of laymen (of one sex) who do not feel out of place in the sanctuary. The 'server class', let alone the 'server mentality', is, I believe, a menace to a true and corporate understanding of the part of the laity in the Liturgy. And, without consciously intending it, we found that this distinction within the laity, between those who were prepared to function in the sanctuary and those who were not, simply disappeared. No one was asked whether he would 'serve'. It was simply assumed that any regular communicant would in his turn take his part in the total action to which all were committed. None of the things that he was asked to do involved anything quasi-clerical or unfamiliar. He might be called upon to read the Epistle. He might be called upon to introduce the biddings or requests for prayer which we as a congregation desired to be included week by week in the intercession of the Church. Above all, he might be called upon, again on behalf of the whole congregation, to make the offering of the bread and wine which represented our common life. This was brought up each week, together with the alms, out of the midst of the congregation. The Offertory is the peculiar liturgy of the laity which no one else can do, since, as we shall insist, it must come from the heart of our every-day life in the world. And just as the bread and wine remain an essential part, and, indeed, the material basis, of the whole eucharistic action, so those who offered them stayed to take their places round the Table until they were joined for Communion by the rest of the laity. They were there simply to *be there*, with nothing peculiar to do that the remainder of the laity did not, to complete the semi-circle which linked the presiding priest and the deacons with the body of the congregation as a whole.

This introduces mention for the first time of a pattern of celebration which I believe to be of fundamental theological, and psychological, importance. At an early stage we took the decision (after one of the best discussions at a Chapel Meeting I can remember and in which the initiative came from a layman) to celebrate across, or better, round the Table, with the president facing the congregation. And from that moment onwards we never contemplated anything else. As I said in the sermon which first explained it, it is a usage which is 'both primitive and Papal and Protestant—and there are not many things of which you can say that! It was general in the early

Church; it has always remained the practice of the Pope himself; it is the regular use in Presbyterian and free churches; and it is being adopted more and more to-day, in Roman Catholic, Anglo-Catholic and Evangelical churches alike. It cuts right across our deplorable party divisions. By burying past contentions, it may point a new way to Church unity; and furthermore, it is a real link with the Church across the centuries.' In the light of more than five years' experience, I would not go back on a word of that. Indeed, it proved in practice a very profound and creative source of unity.

But it is more than that. It is, I believe, of considerable importance for communicating and making articulate the theology of the Eucharist that underlies it. It gives it visual expression in the same way that the right words give it verbal expression. The effect of the eastward position at the Eucharist, with the priest leading the Liturgy with his back to the people, is, pictorially speaking, to focus attention upon a point 'out there' towards which the worship of priest and people is directed. The psychological effect of the westward position is different. It is to focus attention upon a point in the middle, as the Christ comes to stand among his people as the breaker of bread, and to direct their gaze upwards as they lift their hearts to him as their ascended Lord. No one is to say that the one is right and the other is wrong. Each is complementary, and a useful corrective, to the other. But if we recognize that the insights of the Liturgical Movement are calling us in our generation to correct a one-sidedness in our eucharistic thinking, then there is no doubt which of the two is better calculated to recover the sense of one Body created by the one loaf. There is no doubt also which was the pattern of the earliest Christian centuries. But rather than press comparisons, I would simply record that the adoption of the westward position, *with proper theological preparation*, is something which made it a great deal easier for everyone to see and enter into what we were doing with the minimum of verbal explanation.

The criterion of all our experiment was a very elementary one, the test, namely, that St Paul applied to the liturgical situation which he found at Corinth: 'Let all things be done

unto edifying', that is, to the *building up* of the Body of Christ.[1]
Is any given liturgical expression constructive of community,
of *the* community, or does it merely make for individualism?
And when St Paul propounded this test he had something
much deeper in view than simply producing order out of
chaos, or promoting a spirit of fellowship. His purpose has
been well interpreted by Professor Cullmann, when he asks
of the worship of the early Church, 'What was the specifically
Christian *aim* of the gathering for worship?', and answers as
follows: 'The occasions serve for the "building up" of the
community as the *Body of Christ*, the spiritual body of the risen
Lord. The Church as the body of this Christ must take shape
in the gatherings of the community. The Church is built up
in virtue of its coming together. But because the Church,
which is thus built up, is the spiritual body of the risen Christ
himself, we can also say that Christ is shown forth in the
gathering of the community: where two or three are gathered
together in Christ's name, there is Christ in the midst of them
and, indeed, in such a way that he takes form in the gathering
itself. Everything which furthers a "building up", so understood, and only this, belongs to the Christian service of
worship.'[2]

The shape given to the Liturgy will condition profoundly
whether through it is bodied forth the *Totus Christus*, the
whole Gospel for the whole man, or something one-sided or
impoverished. And it is necessary to be clear why, theologically speaking, the emphasis on the corporate character of the
Eucharist is so important. Otherwise the Liturgical Movement
will be betrayed into exalting 'community' or 'fellowship' for
its own sake; and instead of giving theological expression to
the profound Christian mystery that it is participation in the
one loaf makes of us the one Body, it will merely serve as a
cover for the superficial and untheological idea that 'the more
we get together, the closer to God we shall be'.

[1] 1 Cor. xiv. 26. This is, in fact, only one of four tests which St Paul applies in this
chapter and which should be regulative of all liturgy. The other three are: (*a*) 'I will
pray with the spirit, and I will pray with the understanding also' (v. 15); (*b*) If the
outsider or unbeliever comes into your assembly, will he think you are mad, or will
he be compelled to declare that 'God is among you indeed'? (vv. 23-25); and (*c*) 'Let
all things be done decently and in order' (v. 40), an injunction which is grounded in
the fundamental nature of God, as a God 'not of confusion but of peace', and in the
nature of the catholic Church as the embodiment of the one Christ (v. 33).

[2] O. Cullmann, *Early Christian Worship* (S.C.M. Press, 1953), pp. 33 f.

It is perfectly true that the opposite notion, that the further we get from each other (even if only in the pew) the more personal our religion will be, has eaten deeply into our understanding of the Communion, and stands in urgent need of a corrective. For 'solitary religion', as John Wesley wrote in the preface to his hymn-book, 'is directly opposite to the Gospel of Christ. "Holy solitaries" is a phrase no more consistent with the Gospel than "holy adulterers". The Gospel of Christ knows of no religion but social; no holiness but social holiness.' And nowhere is this truth focused more sharply than in Communion, where it is impossible for us to be united to our Head except as we are prepared to be made one with his members. For to participate or share in the Body of Christ is *ipso facto* to be built up into his Body the Church. There can be no communion without community, without *that* community.

But equally it is important to stress that we cannot be united to our fellow members except as we are united to our Head. It is through participation in Christ that we are one with each other, and not the other way round. The great New Testament word *koinonia*, which combines what we are forced to differentiate as 'communion' and 'community', has as its primary reference, in virtually every occurrence,[1] not our fellowship with each other, but our participation in God or Christ or the Spirit. The New Testament knows nothing of generating a feeling of fellowship as a way to God. We are built up into the Body of Christ by feeding upon his supernatural life and in no other way. A religion of 'fellowship' is as much an abomination as 'solitary Christianity'—a truth which Wesley has not had quite as much success in impressing upon some of his latter-day disciples. It is as much a distortion of the *Koinonia* on the one side as are private Masses on the other.

Nor does the corporate character of the Eucharist reside simply in the fact that it is something we must necessarily do together. The theological and liturgical revolution, if it is to be biblical, has got to cut deeper than that. Otherwise there is a danger, which I detect, of all the old clichés being pressed back into service by the simple device of putting them into

---

[1] 1 John i. 3a and 7 are perhaps the only clear exceptions. But cf. in immediate proximity 1 John i. 3b and 6.

the plural. Instead of my coming to make 'my Communion' we come to make 'our Communion', and instead of the priest 'offering the Sacrifice', we come to 'offer our sacrifice'—and all can go on very much as before. But the teaching of the New Testament is not that we can do together what I cannot, but that, *because* of the one loaf, *we who are many* are one Body. The unity is not something from which we can presume to start, except in so far as 'in Christ' we are always and only 'becoming what we are'. The corporeity is something created, or rather recreated, by our participation in the one loaf. By ourselves, even as a group, we are many, fragmented: it is the unity which Christ makes of us, first in Baptism and then in the Eucharist, the unity of the one new Man, that alone gives us the theological right to say 'we'.

Yet there is a sense, important for a Christian doctrine of society, in which the unity of the one new Man is but the restoration, through Christ's new creation, of the natural God-given society of men. It was, I believe, important to try to bring this out in a community such as ours, where a genuine and creative society was still very much a living thing. Those who founded colleges at Oxford and Cambridge were people who understood the biblical truth that it is not good for man to be alone. They established communities (which owed much to the monastic pattern) of men who knew that they could study only if they studied—and lived and worshipped— *together*. And such an ideal was still our heritage, even where it was only half acknowledged. It was this common life—and all that every individual put into it—that lay waiting week by week in the loaf and the cup at the College Communion for Christ's action upon it and through it. And having brought it to Christ—the whole lump of it with its strivings and anxieties and sin—we handed it over to him to take the strain of it (which was only too real at examination time), to bear and take away its sin. And then from him we received back that same bread, that same common life, restored, not merely as the natural bulwark against isolation for which it was created, but as the means of his grace to us. It is important that we should take the sameness of the bread seriously, for all the transformation he works upon it. We come to Communion to receive the Body of Christ. And that means, as well as so much else, the life of the Church in the place where we are. And the life of the Church where we were was the life of a college society restored in Christ to what it was meant to be—the divine healing community, with power to deliver all its members from the isolation and stress that comes from our being too much turned in upon ourselves. There in the common life surrounding us was the means of grace, if we would but let Christ take it and break it and make it *his* Body. Such, in social terms, was the significance of our weekly College Communion.

But everywhere, whether the natural society lies at hand whole or broken apparently beyond recovery, the Eucharist is the clue to the Christian renewal of the social order. Just as this action is the pattern of all Christian action, so the society known here is the pattern of all society redeemed in Christ. The Holy Communion is the great workshop of the new world, where the 'we who are many' are recreated as the true, the new community in Christ. And the holy community known at the Liturgy is only, as it were in inset, the norm of what has to be made true of all society. Here indeed *is* 'the classless society' in which there is neither Jew nor Greek, male nor female, bond nor free. We are not called to 'bring in' the kingdom of God, but to bring it out from where we have known it. Our task is not to 'build' what does not yet exist, but to 'build up' what is already there, that cell of the new society which is present, or should be present, wherever two or three are gathered together in Christ's name. The Communion is social dynamite, if we really take seriously the pattern of community known at the altar. The Church discovered that, in time, in the case of slavery. We have to discover it in terms of race and class and all that is involved for the distribution of the world's resources in the practice, in which we indulge so thoughtlessly each Sunday, of *the absolutely unconditional sharing of bread*.

But this leads directly into a consideration of the third word from which no thoroughgoing theology of the Eucharist can escape.

4. MATTER

If the Eucharist is the most political thing to which the Church sets its hand, it is even more obviously the most material thing for which it comes together. At the very centre stand bread and wine—matter and the sharing of matter. These, one would think, were inescapable; and yet they have been so spirited away in performance of it, and so removed psychologically from any other kind of bread, wine or matter, that the Holy Communion has become in most of our minds the service with the least contact with stuff and muck of this world, and certainly with such unholy concerns as politics and economics, business or finance.

What are we doing when we take, as Jesus did during supper, bread and wine from the table of our everyday lives? We do not ask this question, because in practice that is not what we do. Despite the responsibility which the Prayer Book lays upon the laity, through the churchwardens, of providing the bread and the wine, what in fact happens is that the vicar sends away for a tin of ecclesiastical wafers used for no other purpose whatever,[1] and a bottle of 'sanctuary' wine which no one in their senses would ever drink for pleasure. There is no palpable connection at all between what appears on the credence table and what appears on the kitchen table, between the ecclesiastical vessels in which it is contained, the cassocks and cottas in which it is served, and the world of everyday life. However much clergy may *tell* their people there is, everything they *see* speaks ten times more loudly. How are we to recover the continuity and connection of the Eucharist with an ordinary meal, with ordinary matter, which was such an obvious feature of New Testament Christianity?

It was also, let us remember, a troublesome and shocking feature—and we should not be surprised if it proves so with us. We can only expect that it will not disturb our assemblies if we run away from it altogether, which is what we have done. Nowhere, indeed, in my experience, is the 'offence' of the Eucharist more deeply felt than at this point; and it is especially shocking to laymen whom one might have expected to be the more sympathetic. This offence stems from the completely unreformed, and, indeed, unchristian, conception of holiness, to which I have already referred. Basically it is the Jewish conception of holiness, though, in so far as it is linked with a 'spiritual' depreciation of matter, it is less even

---

[1] As Coslett Quin naughtily says in his admirable book *At the Lord's Table* (Lutterworth Press, 1954), p. 45, the only association of wafers in modern life is with ice cream!

than that. For the Jew the holy was that which was set apart
from the ordinary uses of the world, that which was *not*
common. Indeed, the 'common' was equated with the 'unclean', the very antithesis of the 'holy'. We forget the offence
to the old religion contained in the very name '*Holy Communion*', the *koinonia hagiōn*, 'the making common of the holy'.
To the Jews that meant the desecration of the holy: to the
Christian it meant the sanctification of the common. Such was
the difference which the Incarnation had made, when God
himself had called all things holy; and it is this difference of
which the sacraments are the standing embodiment and
reminder. But for this reason they remain, or should remain,
a standing offence to any mentality that would still like to
drive a wedge between the holy and the common.

In order that this offence may be felt and overcome by faith
it is, I believe, essential that it shall be inescapable. For so long
have we sought, and very successfully sought, to escape it by
insulating the sanctuary from the world, that we are in danger
of destroying all connection between the one and the other.
The Communion has been kept, mentally as well as physically,
in a 'consecrated building', and anything that would not seem
'right' in a consecrated building is 'out'. But we shall never
break through the thought-barrier between the Eucharist and
the secular world, and so liberate the powers of the Eucharist
into the secular world, until we have first removed that barrier
in church. If at the very heart of our religion, in our celebration
of 'the holy mysteries', we enshrine the Jewish conception of
a 'holy of holies', then it will not be the religion of the Incarnation, nor will it know its power. In fact, however, the
Eucharist, far more obviously than any service simply of 'the
Word', is, or should be, the visible denial of any such conception.

The crucial point is the Offertory. People sometimes used
to say to me, 'Oh, you have an Offertory procession, do
you?', as if this were a nice piece of ritual that adds a touch
of movement and colour and 'gives people something to do'.
Nothing could be more irrelevant. We had an Offertory
procession because the Offertory *cannot* start in the Chancel—
or if it does it has lost all its roots in life. The Offertory starts
where the bread and wine start, where our lives are rooted,
in the everyday world of everyday relationships, of family and

society, work and leisure. It is for this reason that the Offertory
is essentially, and not merely by ordering or custom, the
'liturgy' of the laity. For the Eucharist cannot get going, there
is nothing for it to work on, until the world in which the
laity live and work is brought into Church and laid upon the
altar. And it was as a symbol of this that the bread and wine
were brought up each week out of the midst of the people,
from the back of the Chapel, by two members of the congregation. Moreover, if this symbol *is* employed, it is essential that
it shall, as far as possible, speak of that which it is intended to
symbolize. So often its effect is overlaid by its being turned
into a purely ecclesiastical procession, with the Elements
already prepared in chalices and ciboria, and brought up by
servers dressed quite differently from the laity they are sup-
posed to be representing. Normally, indeed, there is no reason
for those who make the offering, any more than for those
who take the collection, to wear anything but their everyday
clothes. In a College we were, however, in a peculiar position.
By ancient custom everyone wore surplices in Chapel, in the
same way that they wore gowns in Hall. To freshmen who
suspected some sinister ecclesiastical significance, I liked to
point out that here, in fact, was a fine witness to the good
Protestant doctrine of the priesthood of all believers! All of
us, laity and clergy, were dressed alike for the Eucharist, the
stoles alone distinguishing the peculiar functions in the liturgy
of the presiding priest and deacons. Again, in the matter of
the Elements, we insisted upon common bread and wine,
brought up on a good secular piece of College plate and in
an ordinary decanter from the butler's pantry. It is, indeed,
also important where possible—and again we were in a
peculiarly fortunate position—that the bread and wine we
offer should visibly represent the life and livelihood of the
local community. And it was for this reason that we had our
loaf baked for us each week in the College kitchens, and used
a bottle of claret, or whatever was available, from the College
cellars.[1] It was but a symbol of the fact that the samples we
offer must genuinely stand for *our* lives, as a community and
as individuals; otherwise it is not our real selves that we are

[1] In an ordinary parish I would suggest that a family be made responsible each
week for bringing (and where possible baking) a loaf, and for procuring a bottle of
wine from the off-licence. This could, if necessary, represent their collection for the
week.

asking Christ to deal with and to consecrate as the materials of his kingdom.

Nor must we burke the fact that what we bring into church are, quite frankly, symbols of the old order, samples of this world with all its sin upon it, of ourselves 'just as we are'. The bread and wine stand not only for what God has given us, but for what we have made of his gifts. To the Eucharist we bring not raw materials, nor even the cultivated wheat and grape, but bread and wine, manufactures, bearing upon them all the processes, and the sin, of commercial production. This is in striking contrast to what we tend to do at harvest festivals, where we load our pulpits and our altars with pears and pumpkins, but steer off the much more questionable manufactures. But the Eucharist does not, like pagan religion, seek to unite us to God through nature unspoilt by man's civilization and sin. It uses for its symbols samples of his very common and often far from holy life, the bread of his penury and the bottle of his excesses. (This used to be brought home rather forcibly when our College Communion followed hard upon the Bump Supper or the Rugger Club dinner of the night before—especially when we had to begin our breakfast by clearing up the bread thrown around and the beer spilt in the previous 'celebration'!) The bread and the wine stand also, of course, for all that is best and freest in life. But, in our legitimate concentration that the Communion loaf shall be 'the best and purest wheat bread that conveniently may be gotten', we have tended to forget that the Prayer Book also requires that 'the bread be such as is usual to be eaten'. And the bread we eat in our world is as much 'the bread of strife' as of anything else.[1] And the more evil we think alcohol is, the more reason why we should use it for Communion. For this is where matter is redeemed, this is where it is recharged and revalued as the carrier of God's new life to men.

[1] Cf. Hosea ix. 4: 'Their bread shall be for their hunger only; it shall not come to the house of the Lord.' Such is the biblical definition of naked materialism, and the greatest judgement the prophet can pronounce on the misuse of matter. This is what the Eucharist exists to redeem and reverse. On this theme, and on others touched upon here, cf. the prophetic chapter (6) in G. A. Studdert-Kennedy's *The Word and the Work* (Longmans, Green & Co., 1931). My attention was drawn to it while this book was in proof by the Reverend A. L. Shands, author of *The Liturgical Movement and the Local Church* (S.C.M. Press, 1959), which I would warmly commend for its own sake and for its bibliography.

It follows from this that the bread and wine of our daily lives are not brought into church to stay there. The Communion is not stamped, like the hymn-books, 'Not to be taken away'. This is obvious, and, indeed, is common property to all Communion teaching. And yet one found that, for those who were shocked that we should bring such secular things into chapel, there were more, initially, who were horrified that we should take such holy things out. The bread and wine set apart and consecrated for the Eucharist itself were, indeed, finished when it finishes, as the Prayer Book directs. But that of the loaf which we had not used we took out to share at the breakfast which followed. Wine in England is rather expensive, and the Bursar might legitimately have jibbed if we had done the same with that, despite the rubric that 'the curate shall have it to his own use'. But the rubric shows that the Prayer Book recognizes the principle: what is broached in church is to be finished outside.

Yet, despite the fact that it is 'bread such as is usual to be eaten', it goes across the grain to smear it with butter and marmalade! Nevertheless, it is only by some such symbol that we may recognize that the barrier *has* been broken down in our own minds, that the Holy Meal is the Common Meal, and that this Common Meal is continuous with every other common meal. Indeed, so powerful is the psychological barrier built up by centuries of thinking of the Holy Communion primarily as a 'service' rather than a meal, that vast numbers of people, I am convinced, are simply not going to 'see' this at all, until they see the Eucharist taken from time to time out of the sanctuary altogether and 'done' on the kitchen table, if necessary with ordinary cups and saucers. (I am certain, incidentally, from experience of considerable discussion, that we shall not otherwise be able to 'get through' to the Quakers at this point, who have preserved for us, but distorted in isolation, so many of insights we need to recover.) But any such proposal raises the spiritual temperature of the average Churchman so abruptly that I merely mention it here *en passant* and shall return to it when there has been time for the resistance to cool. But, by whatever means we must somehow help people to see the connection between this Meal and any other meal; for if they do not see its connection with any other meal, it is certain they will not see its connection with any other matter.

And what we do with matter here has tremendous implications for what we do with matter everywhere. 'When we come together to break bread', said a seventeenth-century writer, 'we must break it to the hungry, to God himself in his poor members'. We cannot without judgement share bread here and acquiesce in a world food distribution that brings plenty to some but malnutrition and starvation to millions more. We cannot without judgement share bread here with men of every race and tolerate a colour bar in restaurants and hotels. In parts of the Christian world, indeed, the logical inference is drawn that white and black cannot meet at the same Communion table; for if they met here they would have also to meet at other tables. Those of us for whom such segregation is a contradiction striking at the heart of the Gospel should ponder equally carefully the implications of being ready to share at Communion what we are *not* prepared to share outside. But do we think that what we do in restaurants, or even at home, really affects what we do at the Communion table or *vice versa*? That was precisely what St Paul was labouring to get the Corinthians to see. For what was the sin of 'not discerning the Lord's body' which made it impossible for them to eat the Lord's Supper? Was it irreverence at the Sacrament, despite done to the consecrated elements? Not that we are told. It was the way they ate their own food beforehand. Each went ahead with what he had brought, and those who had nothing were humiliated (1 *Cor.* xi. 21 f.); they showed they had no 'sense of the Body' (xi. 29, Moffatt). It was their refusal to share bread outside Communion which made it literally impossible for them to eat the bread of life at Communion. For by partaking they could but eat judgement to themselves; they simply invoked upon themselves the very thing their conduct denied, the Body of Christ, the one new Man in Christ Jesus. Have we anything like so integrated a conception of liturgy and life? Oh, if we knew what we do when we come together to break this bread!

That is a conviction which lay very near the heart of everything we felt bound to attempt in our liturgy at Clare. Liturgy 'coming to life' is not merely liturgical revival for its own sake, or even for the Church's sake. It is liturgy coming uncomfortably close to life. For liturgy is nothing less than the gospel of the Word made flesh in action, Christ through his body about his saving work, taking the things of this world and, through the power of his sacrifice, leaving *none* of them untouched.

5. OTHER DEVELOPMENTS

I have tried so far to describe the main stream of development in our thinking and practice. What I have said is not a complete or balanced theology of the Eucharist. I have simply selected certain points upon which we felt it important to place the emphasis, draw out the meaning, or provide a corrective. Some of what has been left unsaid will be found in the sermons and the manual that follows—though there again, naturally, a similar purpose has been at work; for in the very limited space of a liturgical sermon or a sentence or two of comment it is obviously impossible to say everything.

But now I should like to round off this introductory essay with some short observations on certain other developments into which we were led in the course of our concern for these matters. These relate to Baptism, Holy Week, Weekday Communions and the House Church.

BAPTISM

Hitherto the references to liturgy have been almost exclusively to *the* liturgy of the Eucharist; and this reflects the nature of our situation. For one thing, the College Communion was our only Sunday morning service. In the evening we had a shortened Evensong with sermon, which was primarily directed beyond the frontier of those who would call themselves fully-committed Christians. But the Communion and its breakfast was the only occasion for which we met *as the Church* on the Lord's Day. The rest of Sunday morning was deliberately left free for members of the College to join in their different traditions of Christian worship in the city. This focusing of everything upon the Communion was, in fact, a considerable psychological help. It meant that our congregation was not split between a number of services, nor was the Communion relegated in people's minds by being followed by a second service at which the main singing or preaching took place: all was concentrated upon the single central action.

But another effect of this concentration was not so happy. For the Eucharist in our situation was almost completely isolated from the other great Gospel sacrament of Baptism. Admittedly, that is also true in most parishes. But at least there Baptisms are constantly taking place, and the teaching on the one, and even the administration of the one, can be allowed to have some connection with the other. But a College Chapel has practically no Baptisms, and these tend to be domestic rather than collegiate occasions, and often take place in the vacations when Fellows and other senior members bring their offspring to the font. But when a member of the College is baptized, this is by definition an adult Baptism, and it offers a great opportunity.

The majority of those who presented themselves for Baptism were candidates for Confirmation who for some reason or other had not been baptized in infancy. The inevitable tendency was for Baptism to appear merely as a statutory hurdle to be cleared before the candidate could kneel before the bishop, and the pressure was to have the Baptism conducted privately, before the University Confirmation, in the man's own College Chapel.

There is, I believe, a strong case here for a stand, for insisting that adult Baptism, except in exceptional circumstances, should not be administered except as part of the same act as Confirmation. In the case of infants the split is unavoidable: in adult initiation, however, the severing of the theological unity is quite gratuitous. This insistence is not popular because it makes the service longer—though much of the extra-liturgical padding of the Confirmation rite can easily go. But the effect of their combination is to enhance the richness and meaning of Christian initiation beyond measure. The whole becomes a great proclamation of the Gospel, to many who have probably never witnessed an adult Baptism.

But even here the full unity of Christian initiation is still broken. For it is severed from its climax in Communion. The Prayer Book rubric suggesting 'after the Second Lesson or Third Collect at Morning or Evening Prayer' as the right time for Baptism, though laudable in its effort to see that it is done 'in the face of the congregation', in fact seriously breaks the primitive unity in the case of the adult rite.[1] Moreover, the regular practice of administering Confirmation as a separate service in the afternoon or evening quite destroys its conjunction with the Eucharist.

On three occasions we had the opportunity in Clare of celebrating the complete act of Christian initiation as a single liturgical whole. This is now officially recognized as the norm in the revised Baptism and Confirmation services submitted by the Liturgical Commission of the Church of England. But it was possible to achieve the same end by running together the existing Prayer Book services. The Introduction to the Baptism service was modified to form a preamble to the whole rite, and with the omission of the duplications required to make each service a separate act of worship, the whole ran through to reach its climax in the Communion of the entire congregation with its new members. One effect of such a telescoping is to shorten the Confirmation quite drastically in relation to the Baptism, and to reveal it for what it essentially is, the last act of the baptismal liturgy, rather than a second, or even superior, rite. The theological emphasis is laid on the Baptism, of which Confirmation is the crown—which I believe to be both the biblical and the Anglican emphasis—rather than on the Confirmation, to which Baptism is the preliminary.

This experience has convinced me that anything less as the norm of adult initiation is ultimately intolerable. There is no compelling reason why adult Baptism and Confirmation should under usual circumstances ever be separated. Moreover, the administration of Confirmation at the Parish Communion is a desirable and growing practice. And now that we are losing some of our inhibitions about evening Communion, it could spread rapidly on weekday evenings. At any rate in the context of the yearly Confirmation, the primitive and valuable doctrine that the Bishop is ultimately the president at every Parish Eucharist could once again come alive. It is certainly a lesson that bears repetition in that sturdy

[1] It is paradoxical that for infants this time is made purely optional by the addition, 'or such other time as he (the minister of the parish) in his discretion shall think fit', whereas in the case of adults this option is to be exercised only 'if need so require'.

example of Anglican congregationalism, the College Chapel of an ancient University.

HOLY WEEK

I said earlier that one of the disadvantages, liturgically speaking, of a parish subject to the exigencies of the academic year is that the Christian Year is almost completely degutted. Of the major festivals only Ascension Day and Whitsun are left. We tried to make the most of these, having a full College Communion on Ascension Day (which the University still acknowledges, at least negatively, by the intermission of all lectures and examinations) and a specially festive celebration on Whit Sunday. This latter was the one occasion in the year when we had the service at a later hour—at 9.15 or 9.30 a.m. instead of 8 a.m. The time-table of Cambridge life is so tight, even on a Sunday, that so many other things would have become impossible, including our Communion breakfast, if the traditional hour had been abandoned regularly, that we rejected this suggestion after very careful discussion at the Chapel Meeting. Our experience, however, served to show that, except where families are involved (and that is a very big 'except'), the hour makes very little difference: the notion that by merely changing the time and dubbing the service a 'Parish Communion' the revolution is accomplished is a disastrous illusion. But on Whit Sunday we did try to have a service that would as far as possible bring together, as the climax of our year's worship, not only all the undergraduate members of our Society, but the families also of Fellows and the College staff. It coincided more often than not with the end of examinations and the beginning of May Week, and was therefore a naturally festive occasion. In the invitation we sent out to it we used to stress that this was a real 'celebration' in every sense of the word, the baptizing of all the gaiety of the season in the joy of the Eucharist.

Of the other festivals, Christmas, of course, was always in the vacation. But once in an occasional moon Easter falls either in full term or immediately before it. When in a recent year this happened, we took advantage of it to keep the last three days of Holy Week together as a pre-terminal College retreat. And the pattern of it was naturally set by the great drama of our redemption which is spelt out over these those days. Our aim was as far as possible to allow this drama to speak for itself through the action of the Liturgy, whose function precisely is to celebrate and set it forth.

The tendency of all Passiontide devotion is to subjectivize, sentimentalize and individualize. The modern importation (from South American Romanism) of the Three Hours slips very quickly into all these errors, and even at its best leaves completely unanswered the central question: What should the people of God be *doing together* on the day of its redemption to proclaim the Lord's death till he comes? The Prayer Book provision is magnificently objective, unsentimental and corporate; but, as interpreted in contemporary Anglican practice, is concentrated entirely upon the Word.[1] But Good Friday is the day when the Church subjects herself to and proclaims not simply the Word of the Cross (let alone merely the words of Jesus on the Cross), but the Act of the Cross.

This is, indeed, given dramatic expression in the traditional Western rite of the Veneration of the Cross. Here is a profoundly moving piece of symbolic action, as a great wooden cross is exposed before the assembled people of God with the words: 'Behold the wood of the Cross, whereon was hung the world's salvation!' Yet, dramatic though it is and thoroughly evangelical, it must be asked whether this exposition and veneration of the Cross does not belong to that same movement which led in the middle ages to the exposition and veneration of the Sacrament. For in both the 'action' has become a 'thing'. Instead of being thought of as essentially something done, a doing in which we are involved, the memorial of the Cross has become a piece of wood, in face of which we are static.

But the true placarding of the Cross is of the Cross in action. And the act of the Cross is proclaimed and appropriated, as in no other way, in the action by which Jesus first sought to spell out its meaning to the disciples and by which its finished work has been communicated ever since. Indeed, Good Friday is the very day in the year for which the 1662 Prayer of Consecration, with its exclusive focus on the sacrifice of Christ, might specially have been written. And yet it is the one day of the

---

[1] This applies also to the so-called 'Liturgical Three Hours', contrived by running together the Prayer Book offices of Mattins, Litany, Ante-Communion and Evensong.

year, with Holy Saturday, on which by custom, though by no direction of the Prayer Book, it is not used. This is not the place to pursue the historical reasons for this situation, even if I were competent to do so. It is clear that the Prayer Book nowhere orders, nor, indeed, encourages, the practice of stopping with the Ante-Communion; and it appears that this practice as the norm for Good Friday is on any general scale within the Church of England surprisingly modern. The precedents both in our own history and in the other Reformed Churches (in German Lutheranism, for instance, Good Friday is the great day for Communion) need proper investigation. The Roman Catholic Church, in the admirable revision of its Holy Week rites,[1] has now gone as far as restoring Communion from the reserved sacrament on Good Friday. But no arrangement presupposing the use of the reserved sacrament for the regular gathering of the whole congregation (as opposed to the provision for those who cannot be present) is ever likely to commend itself to the Church of England as a whole. Moreover, the explanation given even in the otherwise astonishingly 'reformed' Roman rite, that this is 'a day without a sacrifice'[2] (because Calvary does not need to be 'repeated' this day?) smacks of the worst theology of the eucharistic sacrifice. Is the absence of a celebration on Good Friday more than a rationalization of the historical fact that there were in the early Church no *weekday* celebrations in any case, except, in due course on Maundy Thursday? Weekday communion was from the reserved sacrament, and that on Good Friday came naturally to be taken from what was consecrated the day before rather than on the previous Sunday. It looks as though the original reason for not *celebrating* on Good Friday was the same as for not celebrating on any other weekday.[3]

But whatever the historical causes, there would seem to be strong theological grounds for thinking that if the Eucharist

---

[1] *Holy Week Manual* (Burns & Oates, 1956).

[2] *Op. cit.*, p. 108.

[3] A powerful additional motive has, of course, been that of *fasting*, which is dominant in the letter of Pope Innocent I to Decentius: 'It is quite clear that on those two days the Apostles were both in mourning and hid themselves for fear of the Jews. Moreover, there is no doubt that they fasted on the aforesaid two days to such an extent that the tradition of the Church holds that on those two days celebrations of the sacraments are to be entirely avoided' (Epistle xxv. 4. 7). But this, of course, is an argument against communicating rather than against consecrating and has deliberately been set aside in the Roman restoration of general Communion on Good Friday.

is the memorial *par excellence* of the Lord's death, the memorial that alone makes present what it represents, then it is this—the Cross in action—which, on this day above all days, the Body of Christ should be meeting to show forth to the world—first at the heart of its worship, and then at the heart of its mission. And it does this, in the first instance, *by being itself taken up into the action of the Cross*. This is where the exposition of the Cross, like any representation of it in art or drama or music, must stop short. In the Eucharist the Cross is proclaimed to the world through the Body of Christ himself, as it allows itself to be taken and consecrated, broken and given with its Head for the world's redemption. That, indeed, is an identification and a proclamation which must extend far outside the Liturgy: 'We are always', says St Paul, 'carrying about in the body the death of Jesus, so that the life of Jesus may also be manifested in our bodies' (2 *Cor.* iv. 10). But the liturgy is the point at which this starts, where in the breaking of the bread—of our bread—our lives are conformed to the pattern of his death.

And we come to the Eucharist, as those who have already been baptized into his death and covenanted with him to drink his cup, not simply, like the women, to weep, but, in however muted voice, to make proclamation. We come to celebrate and set forth, in word and in act, the *consummation* of the work of Christ. Hence the note of exultation, of eucharist, is not out of place even on this day. If only from our knees, we must lift up our hearts, and thank him for his death. For, in the words of the traditional Passiontide preface, it is meet, right and our bounden duty that we should indeed give thanks to God who by the tree of the Cross has given salvation to mankind, that whence death arose (i.e. from the tree of disobedience) thence life might rise again. In its proper—and primitive—liturgical expression there is nothing mournful about the celebration of Good Friday. It is stark and bare; but it can never be isolated from the triumph and joy of Easter. Indeed, nothing catches more magnificently the note of *eucharist* proper to Good Friday than the *Pange lingua*:

Sing, my tongue, the glorious battle,
  Sing the ending of the fray;
Now above the Cross, the trophy,
  Sound the loud triumphant lay:
Tell how Christ, the world's Redeemer,
  As a Victim won the day!

We sing that, but on Passion Sunday; and we have tended to transfer to that day a whole aspect of the theology of the Cross which has impoverished and put out of balance our commemoration of Good Friday.

Yet if we are to argue for a Eucharist on Good Friday, it must always be in closest conjunction with the celebrations that precede it on Maundy Thursday and follow it on Easter Day. This unity is safeguarded by the determination to allow the *whole drama* to be conveyed by the action of the Liturgy. Every celebration, indeed, includes the whole in one, on whatever day of the year it is celebrated. But if on these three days the finished work of Christ is spelt out in three successive celebrations, then the manner and style of each can be so adapted as to allow the different 'moments' of it to speak unmistakably, and, indeed, shatteringly, to those involved in it.[1] This is what we tried to do. Nothing could externally have appeared more different than the intimate commemoration of the covenant meal on Maundy Thursday evening, the stark memorial of Christ's sacrifice at noon on Good Friday, and the exultant celebration of the paschal banquet on Easter morning. Yet each brought out and brought home what is included potentially every time we do this to his recalling. What the celebration of the Eucharist on a great festival can do is not only to channel to us and make contemporary for us the mighty act of God it commemorates. It can bring home to us that what we see writ large in *this* celebration is the truth also of *every* celebration. No ferial celebration should quite seem the same again; for in it can be heard, if we have the ear for them, all the multifarious overtones of the high days and holy days.

WEEKDAY COMMUNIONS

What has just been said applies not only to the relation between the festivals and other Sundays, but to the relation between Sundays and weekdays. Weekday celebrations in the Church of England merely reflect the theology, and take

[1] Cf. the excellent discussion of this issue by J. T. Martin, *Christ our Passover* (S.C.M. Press, 1958), pp. 32–7. He points out that, once the primitive practice of celebrating the entire paschal mystery on one night was abandoned in favour of the successive commemoration of its separate moments over three days, logic demands that the single paschal Eucharist should be replaced by three celebrations, 'in which, while the events of our Redemption are recalled seriatim, the action God took in redeeming us is set forth in its wholeness on each day'.

further the practice, of what happens on a Sunday. To put it crudely, in populous or pious areas the filling station is not only open at week-ends: it may even be open daily. That is not in the least to decry the daily celebrations of Holy Communion or the meeting of the people of God to break bread during the week. It is to draw attention, by deliberate parody, to the kind of theology that often underlies them. This theology tends to be the pietism and individualism of the 'simple said service' carried to its logical extreme.

What we should do on a weekday was a question that we were content at Clare to leave till we were convinced what we should be doing on Sundays, and, indeed, by the time I left it was still not fully clear. There was at no time any real demand for a *daily* celebration, which was in any case provided centrally at the University Church. Our inherited practice was to have celebrations on Thursdays and saints' days. Saints' days are, indeed, occasions for celebration. But what, we came to ask ourselves, was the rationale for the Church coming together on a Thursday? It seemed to have as little obvious justification as the practice in the Colossian Church of keeping Sabbaths and new moons, or the special observance of what has been styled that distinctively Protestant festival, the first Sunday in the month. With this question of *when* we should meet, went the more important question of what we should be doing when we did. How were we to close the gap between the theology of our Sunday Communion and our weekday practice? This was put to a committee of the Chapel Meeting on our weekday worship as a whole, and its full recommendation, which was not adopted, is best discussed in the next section. But we began by concentrating our weekday celebrations on saints' days alone, and learning how to adapt our Sunday use to the more intimate gathering of a smaller congregation. Because it is small there is no reason why a celebration should not be just as corporate. And, indeed, the active participation of every member of the Body can be enhanced. What we did was to bring the Table right down into the midst of the congregation, and all gathered round it to receive Communion standing. Latterly, indeed, we adopted the practice, first prompted by our Maundy Thursday celebration, of passing the bread and the cup from one to the other. This is a vivid reminder of the truth involved in every act of communion, that we can have the life of Christ for ourselves only in so far as we are prepared to receive it from our brother and pass it on to our neighbour.

The details are of secondary significance, but the principle at issue here is important. How are we, while keeping our theology whole and constant, to discover what it means to 'do the Eucharist' at every level of the Church's life, from that of 'the great congregation' to the two or three gathered to break bread in Christ's name? For at every level, the *Ecclesia* of God is meeting. Where any come together to do this, there is the whole catholic Church. In 'the great congregation' we have some clues; but in 'the little Church' we have very few. This is largely because those who have rediscovered for us the forms of the Church at this level have tended to be unsacramental in their thinking. The Bible-study group, the prayer meeting, the 'cell' discussion, have brought to life and vitality something of quite inestimable importance for the recovery of the Church at its grass roots. 'The apostles' teaching and the fellowship and the prayers' have indeed been learnt again at the level of the little Church, and largely through its instrumentality. But the other mark of catholicity, 'the breaking of the bread', has come to be recovered only in the more recent revival of the house Church. And this leads into our fourth and last theme.

THE HOUSE CHURCH

It should be said at the start that our concern for this in the context of the College community started where I suspect it always starts, and where our original concern for liturgy started, with evangelism. It was in conjunction with a College mission that we were compelled to ask ourselves how the evangelistic responsibility of the Church in the College could really be brought home to every member of it. This responsibility, like any other responsibility, can be made real only when it is made local, in terms (in our situation) of the neighbour on the same staircase, the friend in the same laboratory or the member of the same team. And yet the evangelistic responsibility of the Christian rests, not upon the individual in isolation (when this is not understood the responsibility becomes over-burdening), but upon the member of Christ in the fellowship of his Church. The smallest unit of distinctively Christian existence—the smallest unit to which the presence of Christ or the fellowship of the Spirit is promised in the New Testament—is the two or three gathered together.[1] We found ourselves therefore driven to break down the responsibility of the Church for the College as a whole to the responsibility of the Christians in the various courts and lodging-houses for those among whom they lived. To *be* the Church there, in all the marks of its apostolic power, was the charge laid upon them. And having begun in prayer, in study, fellowship and planning, it is not surprising that the question in some groups became insistent, 'How can we know each other as the Church at this level without meeting here also for the breaking of the bread?'

I mentioned earlier what an explosive issue this seems to be, especially among laymen. To those who would readily accept sick Communion at home, the idea of bringing the Holy Communion out of a consecrated building, to the level of the loaf on the sideboard and the bottle of sherry in the cupboard, still appears horrific. To those who never think twice about the diocesan Eucharist being broken down into innumerable parish Communions (a step which in the early Church caused considerable heart-searching), the notion that the parish or college Communion should itself be dispersed and localized seems dangerously fissiparous. 'How can it', they ask, 'be anything but sectarian?'—which is exactly the question which the Church of the second century asked, and why it came to insist so strongly upon an apostolic ministry in union with the bishop. There are those again who simply feel that the house celebration cannot be right, others that it cannot be reverent, others it cannot be necessary. But if it is right and reverent and necessary to break *the Word* out of a consecrated building (I almost said 'out of church', but this is to reveal the very identification which causes all the trouble), then it cannot be wrong in principle also to break the Bread. And where necessity is laid upon us evangelistically to rediscover the Church at its most basic level, then, with every proper safeguard, we cannot ultimately stop short of restoring—and one must stress the word 'restoring'—at this level the meeting of

[1] Contrast the Gnostic individualizing version in the Gospel of Thomas, 31: 'Jesus said, . . . Where there are two or one, I am with him'.

Christians for what is after all the heart of the Gospel in action. Let them rediscover its power here, and then, from my experience, they will begin to see visions, not only of the Church and its fellowship, but of the sovereignty of Christ over the secular world, which have been hidden from their eyes by the 'holiness' of the sanctuary.[1]

But no such vision can be forced, and without the unity of the Spirit the Body of Christ can only be destroyed, not built up. So, when such an adventure in churchmanship proved divisive, we preferred to wait. At a subsequent College mission, indeed, it was agreed that any groups that felt called to move forward at this point could do so with the support and authority of the whole Chapel Meeting; but the groups themselves waited for unanimity. The committee already referred to on daily services recommended that, except on saints' days, the normal and proper place for weekday celebrations was at the level, not of the College as a whole, but of the house Church. But this proposal, though it actually commanded a majority in the Chapel Meeting, was too revolutionary a step to push through. Meanwhile, out of the preparation for this second College mission, and as an abiding result of it, the house Church structure came to be a permanent part of the Church in the College. The Chapel Meeting, instead of coming together weekly in one place, met, in much greater numbers, at the level of the staircase groups, uniting only at intervals for policy meetings and corporate instruction. It is of the essence of such groups to split and to multiply among themselves, but their basis remained always the Church in the College. They were not groups of like-minded Christians who drew in others of their own way of thinking. They consisted of those, of whatever difference of background or tradition or denomination, whom the Lord had called to be his Body in that particular area of the College's life. They had not chosen themselves. Nor had any of us. And therein lay our hope. 'Faithful is he that calleth you, who also shall perform it.' And in that promise we were content to wait and to go on, knowing that neither the history nor the theology of such an experiment in the Holy Spirit can ever be closed.

---

[1] See further 'The House Church and the Parish Church' in my book, *On Being the Church in the World*, pp. 83–95.

II
COMMUNION ADDRESSES

COMMUNION ADDRESSES

THE MEANING OF THE EUCHARIST[1]

I. THE ACTION OF THE DRAMA

ON Sunday mornings this term I am going to try and rough out in eight brief addresses what the Eucharist or the Holy Communion is about. (I shall normally call it the Eucharist, the Thanksgiving, simply because this is its most primitive name and puts the emphasis where the early Church did, but substitute for it any other title you prefer.) What is it all about? Let us take as the first clue that lies to hand the two simple words with which Jesus laid this ordinance upon us: 'Do this.' Whatever else the sacrament may be there is no doubt that he thought of it essentially as an *action*, a thing done or enacted—if you like, a drama (which is a Greek word meaning simply 'something done'). I suggest we hold on to this elementary idea of the action, because it will help us to avoid two errors into which experience has shown that Christians easily fall.

The first is to objectify the sacrament as a thing, and to equate it with the elements of bread and wine (as, for instance, in the phrase 'the reserved sacrament'). One then gets tied up in a host of unprofitable questions about the precise relation between this thing or substance and the presence of Christ (theories of transubstantiation, consubstantiation and the rest). And the opposite error is to subjectify the sacrament as a religious experience, or a thing felt. The presence of Christ is again localized, this time inside the believing subject, and if there is no belief then he is not there.

Now I would not worry you with either of these views, which as theories are fairly harmless, were it not that they both lead so easily in practice to an attitude contrary to everything the early Church had to say about the sacrament; I mean an

[1] A course of addresses at the College Communion, first given in the Lent Term 1952 and repeated twice subsequently.

53

individualistic approach to the service in which Communion becomes a number of personal relations to a thing or a number of private religious experiences. The result is that here of all places we get contiguity without community, as each individual comes to make 'his Communion', to establish contact with God on his own private wire.

But if we think of the Eucharist in the first place as an action, we can get away from all this (which is a distortion dating from mediaeval times) back to the intention of Jesus and the early Church. 'Do this'—the verb is a plural one: it is nothing that can possibly be a private affair simply between oneself and God. St Paul introduces his teaching on the Eucharist with the bare words: 'When you come together.' Everyone would understand without being told what that meant. For this was *the* thing for which Christians must come together.

And because we come to *do* something *together*, that in itself answers the question why and when we should go. Most Englishmen would say, I suppose, that the reason why they go, and have been brought up to go, to Holy Communion is to receive personal help and strength for living a Christian life—and everyone of us can testify that that does indeed come. But if that is our primary reason for going, then what has been caricatured as the petrol-pump idea of Communion is absolutely logical. The parson becomes a sort of garage proprietor whose job is to be open (weekly, monthly, daily, according to demand) for any of his customers who require to fill up. Who comes and how often depends, quite naturally, on what the individual thinks he needs and how much he feels he gets from it.

But try now to see the Eucharist as the New Testament saw it, as *the* corporate act for which the community must come together, and the matter cannot help looking rather different.

Let us go back to the beginning. By Baptism we were, so to speak, signed on (and at Confirmation we were put in the cast) as actors in a great company, whose very *raison d'être* is to present to the world—or rather to let Christ present through it—the drama, the finished act, of its redemption. That is what as Christians we are on the stage of this world for—not merely to run through the tragi-comic turn of the seven ages of man, but to present to men what Dorothy Sayers called 'The

Greatest Drama Ever Staged'. This presentation is no mere play-acting: it is a proclaiming, a making present, of the Lord's death, of his whole redemptive act, till he comes, bringing it to bear in saving efficacy upon the here and now.

And the way in which Christ gave instructions for this to be done was quite brutally simple. The Church, as now his body, was to reproduce it, to placard it, in its own life—by allowing itself like him to be taken, itself like him to be consecrated to God's purpose, itself like him to be broken in sacrifice, itself like him and through him to be released in triumph for the world's redemption. Christians are to be the presentation in time, the moving picture, the body, of the suffering and victorious Christ. It is this pattern of obedience, this four-fold action cycle, that we come to the Eucharist, first to live through and then to live out. We come, together to do this, together to have this done to us—to let Christ take us, and sanctify us, and break us, and make us the instrument of his world-conquest. Everything else—the prayers we say, the words we use, satisfaction of personal need—is secondary.

This is the action, the spring and the pattern of all other Christian action, for which Sunday exists, and by which alone it was for centuries distinguished from every other working day. This is the drama for which every Christian is cast, and for which all other prayer and all other worship is rehearsal. It is Christ's *command* performance. And it should be as unthinkable for any full member of the Church simply to cut this corporate act as for someone in a West End company to decide one evening to take the night off. Anyone responsible for amateur dramatics knows that nothing plays such havoc with a show as absenteeism from rehearsals, let alone from the night itself. Well, this is the night itself, the Church's moment, when on the Lord's Day the Body of Christ does for the world what its Lord commanded and places itself in his hands for death and life. The question still, I surmise, put to Confirmation candidates, 'How often should I go?', is as if the disciples had asked *that* night, the night in which he was betrayed, 'Need I be there?' There was one only who could think of leaving that evening, and when he went out it was night indeed.

2. THE COMPANY

I tried last week to make the single point of the Eucharist as *action*, and of Christ as present, not as a thing on the altar nor simply as an experience in the heart, but as an agent, the doer, the breaker of bread, the host at supper. In the action of the Eucharist it is he that takes, he that blesses, he that breaks, he that gives—or it is nothing. Yet equally it is, on his own instruction, our action: 'This do ye.' Perhaps the best way of expressing it is to say that the Eucharist is the action of Christ in his Body, his action through us for the world. We are the company chosen for his command performance, and in this performance each of us has his part, or, as a first-century Christian writer described it, his 'liturgy', or piece of public service.

Let us spend a little time this morning getting clear what this means. It sounds perhaps rather obvious, but in the manner of our performance, and therefore in our thinking about the service, it has got heavily overlaid and obscured. For instance, if someone were to ask you after this service, 'Who celebrated this morning?', you would say, 'Oh, the Chaplain'—for that is how we now use the word. The celebrant is the priest, everyone else is 'the congregation', for whom he celebrates. Apart from joining the minister in some of the prayers, the outward activity of the laity is normally confined to receiving. The main action of the drama—the 'doing' of the Eucharist, as the early Church called it—is concentrated in the hands of one man. This change, from the Eucharist as the corporate action of the whole body of the Church to something done by the clergy for the people, was a mediaeval development. It set in with the introduction in the West (it has never happened in the East) of low Mass, familiar to us as 'the simple said service' celebrated by a single priest for a relatively passive congregation, which most of us assume to be the norm of what the Communion service is. This concentration of the whole eucharistic action in the hands of one man was not seriously affected by the Reformers, for all their stress on the priesthood of all believers. In fact, it was carried further. At a typical Reformed Communion service the laity have nothing to say at all; the minister says and does everything, including the confession.

We shall not really understand the Eucharist as the joint action of the whole people of God unless we get beneath this layer of clericalization. Perhaps we can see it better if I simply try to describe the kind of pattern a primitive Eucharist, say of the second or third century, would have followed—not that we want in the least to write off or undo Christian history since, but simply because here the essential corporate action stands out clear and unadorned.

The service would, of course, take place not in a church but in a private house, under conditions of considerable secrecy and danger. But the setting is here irrelevant. The person presiding (normally the bishop of the local community) would stand behind the table, flanked in a semi-circle by the presbyters, facing the people. The Eucharist proper would normally be preceded by the *Synaxis*, or Liturgy of the Word, which included readings (interspersed by psalms) from the Old Testament and the new Christian writings, and a sermon. After this anyone who had not been baptized would have to go, and the Ante-Communion would conclude with the intercessions of the faithful. But these would not have appeared to us much like our corresponding prayer for the Church militant, which in form is now a clerical monologue to which the congregation says 'Amen'. Rather, like everything else, the praying was a corporate act of the Church—one of the things for which the worshipping community existed—and everyone had his indispensable part in it. The deacon would introduce the biddings; there would follow a silence in which the real body of the praying was done—by the people; finally, the bishop or whoever was presiding would draw it all together in a collecting prayer, or collect. The deacon would then give out another subject for intercession, and so on. (Our conception of public prayer is for the most part these headlines or collects strung together and put in the mouth of one man.)

After the intercessions there would be a break, and the eucharistic action itself would begin—with the kiss of peace. If you could not exchange this with the man next to you you had no right to be present. Everyone would then come up to the table bringing a roll of bread and a little flask of wine (with other contributions in kind), which would be received on a salver and in a large loving-cup held by the deacons. What was needed for the service was then placed on the table, and the president and presbyters would each add their own. Then, in silence, he and they stood with their hands outstretched over the offerings. After the dialogue which forms the oldest part of our present service ('Lift up your hearts...', 'Let us give thanks (or make eucharist) unto our Lord God...'), there followed the Prayer, the only prayer in the Eucharist proper, which was the president's own particular liturgy on behalf of the Body. This was the prayer of Blessing or Thanksgiving, to which St Paul may well allude (1 *Cor.* xiv. 16) and which probably goes back to the prayer Jesus, as head of his little family, would have used over the cup at the Last Supper. To this everyone replied with a solemn and triumphant 'Amen', which again St Paul mentions (1 *Cor.* xiv. 16). There followed a pause, as the president broke one of the rolls. He ate a piece himself and sipped from the cup, and as he gave to those at the table with him the deacons broke the rest of the rolls for distribution. Then one of them came forward with him and they stood out in front of the table. Everyone filed up and, still standing, received a piece of the bread, before passing on to sip the cup held by the deacon. In each case the communicant's own reply of 'Amen' sealed the words of administration. Then abruptly to the dismissal, and without unnecessary loitering people slipped off home in twos and threes through the back door.

From beginning to end the action, swift and direct, was the performance of the whole company, and in it everyone had his own part or liturgy, without which the others were incomplete. The whole was a great concelebration or symphony of action.

It is a paradox that the Communion of all acts of worship has tended in the course of time to become the least communal or congregational. But this is essentially the people's service, *the* public service rendered by the people of God. And we shall be missing something very near the heart of the whole if we never feel what it means to be cast for an active part in this great dramatic company, which one of the early Fathers called the *plebs sancta Dei*, the holy common people of God.

3. THE PRESENTATION

One of the things that will always stick in my memory is being asked to celebrate for the small community of Anglican visitors to Oberammergau on the morning of the Passion play. In an hour or two's time we were to share in what must remain for anyone who has seen it one of the spiritual experiences of a lifetime. Into that presentation of the Passion was to be put everything of which man was capable—all the resources of a village with three hundred years of tradition, devotion and technique behind it. Into the vast theatre would pour over 5,000 people that morning from literally the ends of the world. Yet beforehand in the simple white-washed Lutheran church, considerably smaller than this chapel, something was happening that was greater than any of it. Another passion play was in progress—and in the difference between them lies the clue to the Eucharist. Here the actors were not merely human beings, however dedicated, but Christ himself in his risen Body. And this presentation was not simply play-acting, a miming of our redemption, however consummate. It was itself an integral part of that redeeming activity. Here was Christ actually about his saving work, channelling into the present moment all that was finished, yet only begun, on the Cross. In the simple actions round that table was all the efficacy of Calvary itself. What was done for us, soon to be represented so dramatically on the stage, was here and now being wrought in us.

When we come to the Eucharist we come not simply to a representation of something that has happened, as in the Oberammergau play. We come to be present at—and at the same time to present, to transmit to the world—something that is happening. Here at this service we enter the very workshop of the new world. Here the master carpenter is in action, refashioning matter and men, forming and tooling the Body which is the instrument of his mission. When we have been to Communion we have been present at the changing of the world, present at the carpenter's bench, yes, and on the carpenter's bench, so that our whole lives come out chiselled and renewed. Here, to illustrate the point, are some words written of a Mass celebrated at the end of a day by a priest-workman in a docker's home in France: 'The mystery of the

Redemption is taking place at the very spot where it is needed. Outside, the seven children of the Valès family are playing, and when after our thanksgiving we meet in the court all hung with drying linen and old blankets being aired, life seems new to everyone.'

It is this new life that the Eucharist is proclaiming, making present, in the world and for the world. And it does this because it is what Jesus himself called 'my recalling', literally, 'the *anamnesis* of me'. It is a word seriously undertranslated by our word 'remembrance', which inevitably suggests for us the mere mental recollection of something absent. But in biblical usage the word means the bringing back of something out of the dead past, so that it becomes actually effective here and now. The stress is on presence rather than absence. The Eucharist is a re-presentation (not a repetition), a making presently operative, of all that was done 'once' for us and our redemption. It is that of which our Consecration prayer speaks when it records that Christ 'did institute, and in his holy Gospel command us to continue, a perpetual memory of that his precious death, until his coming again'. This particular phrasing conveys the unfortunate suggestion that while he is absent this is the best we have to be going on with. Rather, it is here that he is present, that he comes to his own, that according to his promise he eats bread and drinks wine new with us in the kingdom of heaven, here that, in the words of the Epistle to the Hebrews, we taste, already in this old order, the powers of the age to come.

To-day is the feast of the Presentation of Christ in the Temple. There could hardly be a better description of the Eucharist. Here, in the temple of his Body, the Christ is made present, and is presented to the world, in all the power of his death and risen life. The Eucharist is the great epiphany or manifestation of Christ, standing between his first showing forth to the world in Herod's temple and his final epiphany in the clear glory of his finished creation, the new Jerusalem. It sets forth his work for the world and it sets it forward, as week by week the Christian community, in the place in which it is set and for which it is answerable, invokes over the bread and wine and all the relationships of our present life the redeeming acts of Christ—and yet another bit of this old order is taken, and blessed, and broken, and transformed. Here, indeed, is the very theatre of salvation; this is the molten moment of the new creation, that new continuous creation, which was begun in the crucible of Golgotha and which goes forward till all things are made new.

4. ACT I—TAKING

On the last three Sunday mornings we have, as it were, set the stage. We have looked at the action of the drama, we have been through the cast, and seen what it is we join to present. And now, after the Liturgy of the Word, which, like the overture, sets the mood of the performance with the change of the seasons, we come to the first Act—the offertory or the taking of the bread and wine, the raw material of the eucharistic action. In itself this may seem merely a tedious preliminary (like laying the table) to be got out of the way as quickly and unobtrusively as possible. And, indeed, the manner in which it is usually done would seem to confirm this way of regarding it. It has become just one of the motions gone through in the sanctuary while the congregation are otherwise engaged, in taking the collection or singing a hymn or simply burying their heads in their hands. But as long as the Eucharist was thought of as the corporate act of the whole Body, the offertory was one of the four great moments of the Action, every bit as important as any of the others. In the eastern Orthodox Church to-day the Great Entrance, as it is called, when the bread and wine are brought in in procession, forms one of the climacterics of the service—indeed, as far as the laity are concerned, this and the distribution of the elements are the only acts of the drama they see, as the rest goes on behind an impenetrable screen. From primitive times the offertory was felt to be the special liturgy of the laity, their peculiar contribution, which no one else could make, to the whole symphonic action. This survives to-day in the use in many churches of a server to hand the priest the bread and wine; in the fact that in a parish it is the responsibility not of the vicar but of the churchwardens to supply the materials for the Holy Communion; and, of course, in the collection at this point of alms— the continuation in monetary form of the gifts in kind brought for the common use, *out of which* was set apart the bread and wine needed for the service.

Now it is no accident that this particular movement of the Action should be the special charge upon the laity, for it is a movement that must have its origin in the very heart of the everyday world of work and leisure. It was 'as they were eating' that Jesus took bread from off the table. And in the offertory we are simply taking a dip into the world and lifting out of it a sample of the common livelihood of man—a loaf of bread and a bottle of drink: not corn and wine, not raw materials (as in Baptism, where the water represents the sheer action of God towards us, to which we contribute nothing), but products, tokens both of God's creation and of man's labour upon it. Into that loaf of bread goes the whole working life of the world—all the complicated processes of production, distribution and exchange. And in the bottle of wine we have the symbol of all life's joy and leisure, everything given to make glad and free the heart of man. All that we take, as it were, off the table of our daily lives, and we place it in the hands of Christ for him to transform and use. In the bread and wine we bring is handed over to God all we are, everything he has made us and everything we have made ourselves. As the offertory goes up, we say in effect: 'There you are, God— my brains and my brawn, my friendships and contacts, all we are and do together in this community, the whole teeming activity of our College and University life—take it and use it for the extension of your reign, here and to the ends of the earth.'

The offertory is the thrust of the secular into the very heart of the sacred. It should not start in the sanctuary—if it does our religion is losing its roots in the stuff and muck of life. It starts wherever the people of God find themselves during the week, in factory and office, laboratory and common room. That is why we and increasing numbers of others have revived the old practice by which the bread and wine to be used for the service are brought up by representatives of the laity from the west end of the Chapel. And what we bring into the sanctuary is a loaf of bread from the College kitchens and a decanter of wine from the College cellars—the point being that the offertory should as far as possible genuinely express and represent the daily life of the community that makes it. For what we do in this action is to bring the world—our world—into the Church, just as at the end of this service we have to take the Church out into the world. The new community, the Body of Christ, is made out of the same materials as the old. And if the universal claim of Christ's kingship means anything, it means that there is nothing in the secular order, however profane, which has not got to be made material for consecration. What we are doing at the offertory is simply letting God get his hands on it, or that of it which is represented by our lives, so that through us, his new community, the whole world with which it is in contact may ultimately be changed. 'Behold the handmaid of the Lord; be it unto me according to thy word.' If a village girl had not thus been prepared to hand herself over to God's will, there would, humanly speaking, have been no Christmas Day and no new world. And so it is with God's kingdom to-day. It depends on lives, ordinary lives, put unreservedly at its disposal, the five barley loaves and two small fishes of this lad here and that one there, out of which the miracle of the new creation can be wrought.

5. ACT II—BLESSING

Last week we considered the action of the offertory, what I called the thrust of the secular into the heart of the sacred, when the symbols of our daily work and leisure are taken off the table of our lives and handed to our Master as the materials of his new society. I made the point that the bread represents all the energies and productivity of man brought to bear upon the work of God, the wine all the joy and refreshment of life distilled, if you will forgive the mixed metaphor, from the overflowing bounty of God. Every celebration of the Eucharist is a sort of harvest thanksgiving, when all that we have been and all that we have done during the past week is brought to Christ—the very fabric of our lives here in the loaf and in the cup.

Yet everything that we have been and done is scarcely material for thanksgiving. Bread, as the sample of man's production, represents not merely fair work and honest labour, but a good deal of laziness and graft, profiteering and self-seeking, and a world distribution bringing plenty to some but deprivation and malnutrition to many more. And the

bottle, as well as providing the wine of life, has become a
by-word for some of the most tragic forms of degradation and
misery and moral collapse. The world is, indeed, as Gerard
Manley Hopkins wrote, 'charged with the grandeur of God'.
But

> Generations have trod, have trod, have trod;
> And all is seared with trade; bleared, smeared with toil;
> And wears man's smudge and shares man's smell.

Our largely sentimental harvest festivals contrive to conceal
this by concentrating on turnips and pumpkins, where the part
of man is at a minimum, and cutting out the much more
questionable manufactures. I remember once preaching at a
harvest festival in a small Somerset town whose whole popula-
tion virtually was employed in a shoe factory—but there was
not a shoe in the church. And if certain parishes in Liverpool
were really to bring the harvest of *their* work (and not someone
else's), you probably would not see the altar for pool forms.
And nothing might be better calculated to show up the true
valuation and direction of much of our life.

At the offertory we are showing our hand—the talents God
has given us and what we have made of them. There is no
sentimentality about the Eucharist. The bottle and the loaf
we bring are quite frankly symbols of an old, unredeemed
world, of much work in the past week skimped and shoddy,
of much leisure frittered selfishly or uselessly away. Before
they can become symbols of the new they must be raised to a
fresh level. And this is what happens in the second Act that
we are thinking about this morning, the act of blessing or
consecration.

When Jesus took the bread and the cup, he blessed, or gave
thanks. By this action, by setting them in the true relation to
God in which he himself stood, he restores them to become
what all matter was meant to be, and, renewed in Christ,
must one day become—the direct means of contact between
God and man. Identified with Jesus, the only whole and normal part of God's creation, these forestalments, as it were, of
his finished work can even now give us a share in his new
creation. They are charged afresh with the grandeur of God
and the quickening powers of the resurrection life. From being
merely symbols of the old order, they become revalued as the

vehicle, the body, of the living Christ. He redeems them from the world's uses and releases them to perform their true function of carrying his own, eternal life to man. Brought into relation with him, fused with his personality, our lives (summed up in the bread and wine) are thus given back to us, no longer simply our own but his Body, members of his redeemed and redeeming community. We go out from this service identified with Jesus Christ, men, as the great Brighton preacher, F. W. Robertson, put it, 'in whom the resurrection begun makes the resurrection credible'. Over our lives have been spoken the consecrating, transforming words: 'This (of yours) is *my* body and blood, *my* life.' Here is the beginning point of the transformation which has to be wrought out, first in us, and then through us, till the whole body of this old world becomes conformed to the likeness of Christ's glorious body.

Sunday and its worship may appear like a break and respite from the hard practical business of life. Yet of all earthly things upon which we can be engaged the Eucharist is the most practical. Do we really want a new and better world? Then this is the great solvent of the old, transforming it by divine alchemy into the new. Here, rather than at death, is where the resurrection of the body begins. It is here that 'this corruptible' (the whole body of sin and death we know) begins to 'put on incorruption', here, in this anticipation of God's new world, that we start the process, which St Paul says we all must go through in the end, of being 'changed', as week by week we are fashioned anew into the Body of Christ, which is both the pledge and the instrument of all creation's destiny.

6. ACT III—BREAKING

We come now to the third of the four actions of Jesus at the Last Supper which fix the structure of the Christian Eucharist. This seems to have been one that most vividly impressed itself upon his disciples. It was in his manner of breaking the loaf that he was recognized by his friends at Emmaus, and, together with the element of thanksgiving or eucharist, the breaking of the bread was so dominant a part of the Action that it could naturally come to stand as a name for the whole. In itself the breaking is a simple and insignificant process required purely for the purposes of distribution—like cutting the loaf at meals. But it would hardly have assumed such controlling significance if that is all Jesus and his followers saw in it. In fact, taken with the identification of the cup with his outpoured blood, it was surely intended by Jesus as a symbolic act, to enable them to enter into the real meaning of the death he was shortly to accomplish. This was to be the true significance of the Cross. By this dramatic action he was imposing upon what outwardly would appear nothing but a common judicial murder the character of a self-sacrifice, undertaken consciously and voluntarily, to inaugurate an entirely new relationship between God and man. 'Look', he is saying, 'this is my body which *I* am breaking, this is my blood which *I* am giving, for the world's redemption'.

And when he told his friends to 'do this', when he enjoined this action upon us, he bound us along with him to the same self-sacrifice. Last week we saw how in the act of consecration or blessing our lives are fused with his divine life and are made one with his body. But his body, while evil remains in the world, is a racked and suffering body. And it is to this that we are committed. Our self-identification with Christ in the Eucharist is rather like letting ourselves be coupled to the great driving wheels of an express train. That means power—the very power behind the universe becomes transmitted to us. But it means that the pace and direction of our lives are no longer simply ours to control. And it means, maybe, that we shall be broken on that wheel before our service is out.

The breaking, the blood—that is sacrifice. And sacrifice is not a pretty thing; in fact, it's a thoroughly beastly business, and it's dynamite to touch. So if you want to retain a nice, quiet idea of the Communion you had better switch off now. . . . Otherwise you will follow me through into an extermination centre. There is a mass execution in progress. The executioner's assistant is counting heads as the victims file into the death chamber. When he has accounted for the lot, he hands them over to the officer in command, and the doors on the outside world shut with a final click.

Perhaps you recognize the scene—for it comes from the Communion service. You have just passed through the fore-chamber of the Ante-Communion, and, with the offertory over, the doors on the world outside are shut. The deacons set apart so much bread and so much wine, for each person present, and as they hand it over to be laid upon the altar it is separated for ever from the uses of this world. There awaiting their death are the lives of fifty or more young men, summed up in an ounce or two of bread and half a pint of liquor. That is what they had of God, and that is what they made of it. There it goes, laid upon the block, covered with its shroud. There we go. And as we await the end we say our last prayer for the world, make our confession and receive our shriving. Then swiftly the action moves to its climax. We have given Christ our lives, we have let him make them one with his; then he takes them in his hands—and he *snaps* them. And lastly, as in some grim parody of a suicide club, his desperadoes drink the cup of death together, pledging their lives to flow with his for the establishment of his kingdom. There the parallel stops. For this cup of death is also the cup of life, and the act of Communion resurrection from the dead. The forces of the risen life are released, and a hang-dog collection of condemned men becomes galvanized into the new community of the Body of Christ.

But before communion, the breaking, the fraction. The new life is to be lived and a new world built only in the power of sacrifice, in the incalculable power of his sacrifice. In this service we come to lay hold on that and let it take hold of us. I was present some years ago at the chapel of a theological college where we gathered for Communion round an altar that was simply a bare stone slab and looked for all the world like a chopping block. It was cold; it was merciless to the emotions. But after all, if there is not something of that about our religion, if the block of sacrifice is not near its heart, it will soon become flabby and useless. We come to this service not to get a jag of anaesthetic to put us on another week. We meet to bind ourselves in death and life with him who came to cast fire upon the earth. And that cannot stop here, in church. Once the fuse to a stick of dynamite is lit, you must throw it or be blown.

7. ACT IV—SHARING

And so we reach the last of the four great moments of this dramatic Action—the sharing together of the bread and wine that Christ has taken, blessed and broken. 'Take and divide it among yourselves', he said. 'Eat this.' 'Drink ye all of it' (not, as the Greek makes clear, 'all of it', but 'all of you drink'). The ring of fellowship is closed as those whom Jesus has just called his 'friends' pass the cup round for the last and most intimate time. Yet this fellowship is not simply the old made more significant by circumstance. The purpose of this meal, says Jesus, has been to initiate a new covenant relationship, shortly to be sealed and ratified in his blood. Just as God's people of old was brought into being by the covenant sacrifice at Sinai, so this insignificant band of twelve working men was here being created the nucleus of the new people of God, whose life was to spring from his death. The Last Supper was the dress rehearsal for the first supper of the new age, when the risen Lord would with them eat the bread and drink the cup new in his kingdom, and life would begin afresh in the resurrection order brought into being by Good Friday, Easter and Whitsun.

The common sharing of the loaf and cup, made new by their association with his life, was what was to bind them together as the new community. That is what St Paul means when he says, 'Because there is one loaf, we who are many are one body'. The Eucharist is that which creates, and constantly recreates, the Church. Because it is what enables us to partake of the Body of Christ, it is what makes us parts of the Body of Christ. The divine life we share is essentially a corporate life. It is one and the same Greek word, *koinonia*, which we translate variously as participation, communion, fellowship, community. That is why St Paul says to those at Corinth whose individualistic practices show they have no 'sense of the Body', the Church, that they can only eat and drink the Eucharist to their own condemnation. For in it they are receiving, inviting in judgement upon themselves, the very thing their lives deny— the life of the one new Man in Christ Jesus. For this reason breach of fellowship is *par excellence* what excommunicates— for breaking *that* Fellowship is dividing, dismembering Christ himself. And as St Paul said, and in saying it no doubt shocked and puzzled his converts, breach of fellowship includes not only open animosity and conscious schism but sheer individualism.

I have put this strongly—though no more strongly, I think, than the New Testament itself puts it. But, by way of balance, let me now make equally strongly a point which may appear the absolute contradiction of it. I can put it most succinctly perhaps by reminding you of the fact that it is precisely at this point in the service—the moment when its essential corporate nature presses more inescapably than anywhere else—that for the first and only time in our liturgy the words 'we' and 'our' yield place to the singular 'thee' and 'thy'. 'The body of our Lord Jesus Christ, which was given for *thee*, preserve *thy* body and soul unto everlasting life. Take and eat this in remembrance that Christ died for *thee*.' What we receive as we kneel round the Table is our *own* share in Christ's death and life, our own involvement in it, which can be ours and no one else's. It is a present with our own name upon it, from him who divides to each severally as he wills and knows his own by name. Indeed, I have taken part in a liturgy where the words of administration were, very impressively, preceded in each case by the individual's Christian name: 'John, the body of our Lord Jesus Christ; Mary, the blood of our Lord Jesus Christ . . . for thee.'

But significantly enough that particular liturgy was written and designed precisely to bring out the social and corporate nature of this fellowship act. It is one of the deep mysteries of the truth as it is in Jesus that there is no contradiction or even antithesis here between the personal and the social. My personality is most whole, most free, most truly my own, when and as I come to find myself *in* Christ, which means inextricably for the New Testament in the Body of Christ, the fellowship of the redeemed. What I receive in Holy Communion is something that makes me fully and victoriously a person such as I can never be when left to myself: but it does it by making me a 'member', part of a body. What is 'given for me' is a share in a company, my share with my own unique name upon it, but something that will bear interest for me only as the company flourishes. One cannot have Christ apart from his Body, and in practice the power of Christ in any individual's life will depend very largely upon how dynamic is the Christian community of which he is part. Recognizing this, we meet here to take to ourselves this transforming power of Christ in his Church, to let our separate lives be knit up and restored as members of his Body. The bread which we break, is it not a sharing in the Body of Christ?

United with him, as St Chrysostom said, 'we become one single body, limbs of his flesh and bone of his bone. This is the effect of the nourishment he gives us'. And because of this St Augustine could say to his people: 'It is your mystery that you receive. You hear the words, "The body of Christ", and you answer [as each person used to on receiving, and is still required to in the Scottish liturgy], "Amen". Be therefore members of Christ, that your "Amen" may be true. . . . If you have received well, you are that which you have received.'

8. EXIT

Perhaps you have thought it odd at the climax of a course for there to be a whole sermon devoted to the word 'Exit', which is, after all, just a stage direction necessary to get the players off. Such a stage direction, or rubric as it is called in liturgy, does in fact occur, and has got into the text, in the Roman order of the Communion service: 'Ite, missa est'. In origin it is a purely secular formula, equivalent to: 'You can go now, the meeting is over'. It is ironical that it should have given rise to what most people would regard as the most ecclesiastical name for the service, 'the Mass', and curious, too, that what amounts to the word 'exit' should have become the title of the drama itself. But even this otherwise meaningless title of the Mass can perhaps be of some use if it reminds us (as admittedly it usually does nothing of the sort) that the point of the Action really begins where it finishes, that its effectiveness is bound up with its closing note: 'Get out!' What begins with 'Draw near in faith' must end with 'Arise, let us go hence'—and both movements are equally vital, or the world will not be changed. When Jesus spoke those latter words to end his discourse in the Upper Room, it was to go out to make real *for* the world the sacrifice whose meaning he had just spelt out at supper. For us they come as a command to go and make real *in* the world what he has done for us and to us in this fellowship meal. Because we have been here this morning, and identified ourselves with the bread and wine, over everything that we are and everything we shall touch and do during the coming week will have been pronounced the words, 'This is my body . . . This is my blood'. As soon as the service is over, we have to get out and make that effectively true. If the bread and wine are not genuine *samples*, if the only bit of the old world that is re-created by Christ is inside a church building, then the sooner we join some other society that really does get into the world the better.

As Christians, we have this Action at the centre of our religion because we believe that there is no other way in which the world and human nature can be changed and reduced to the sovereignty of God. Even for Christ himself there was in the end no other way. That is the meaning of Gethsemane. If God's kingdom were ever to become a reality in the lives and societies of men, he had himself to be taken and handed over to death; he must be willing to be consecrated wholly to the Father's will; he must be broken and poured out in sacrifice; only so could he communicate to men the power of his new life. It was this that he was finally trying to demonstrate to his disciples over supper by those mysterious actions with the loaf and cup which he identified with himself. And by making these actions something that they too were to do, he showed there was no escaping this pattern this side of the final victory. In this age, if God's kingdom is to be established, it will only be through persons ready with him and by him to be taken, blessed, broken, and released in power. Listen to St Paul's description of Christians in this world as people 'always carrying in the body the death of Jesus, so that the life of Jesus may also be manifested in our bodies. For while we live we are always being given up to death for Jesus' sake, so that the life of Jesus may be manifested in our mortal flesh'. There is the eucharistic pattern in motion, with its rhythm pervading the whole being of those who by Baptism have been grafted into Christ. The Church is the body in which his surrender and consecration, his dying and living, are constantly being carried around. That was the instinct—the true instinct—which led in the Middle Ages to the carrying of the Blessed Sacrament in procession through the streets. It was a witness to the fact that the action of the Eucharist (however obscured by its identification with the thing, the elements) is not something that can possibly stop in church. As it begins, in the offertory, with the thrust of the secular into the heart of the sacred, so it ends with the releasing of the sacred into the midst of the secular.

In the prayer of thanksgiving after receiving, we ask that we may 'continue in this holy fellowship' or communion. 'Continuing in the Holy Communion' is an admirable description of the Christian life. In so many churches one has the impression that it is marked, like the hymn-books, 'Not to be taken away'; and directly people set foot outside the door they slip off home without a word or a smile, oblivious apparently of having just been bound up in the strongest fellowship the world can ever know. But if we are alive to what has here been done to us, it must issue in two things. First of all, we must *meet*, to let this fellowship find its expression outside church. That is why we go straight out from this holy meal into a common breakfast. And in the Chapel meeting and its groups we join again to translate into thought and action all that it means to be the Body of Christ, the people of the mission, which this shared act has made us. The Communion, the meal and the meeting are really all (as they were in the first century) parts of the same thing, of the Church coming together to *be* the Church in and to the world in which it is set. But, secondly, to take this Holy Community out with us, we need not only to meet but to scatter—carrying into every part of our common life and society the transforming powers of the new world we have here known. This outgoing commitment is bounded only by the ends of the earth and the end of the age. For every Communion looks forward to the moment when 'sacraments shall cease', when we shall no longer, as now, be living in two worlds, but the kingdoms of this world shall have become the kingdom of God and of his Christ. Every celebration is bounded and orientated by the words, 'Till he comes', just as each Jewish Passover ends still on the note of expectancy: 'Next year in Jerusalem!'.

PREPARATION FOR COMMUNION[1]

I want to talk this morning quite simply and directly about preparation for Communion. I confess that I have always found this something extraordinarily difficult. And part of the reason I believe is this—that we have been brought up to view the thing too narrowly, as preparation simply for the individual act of receiving Communion. Moreover, the assumption on which the traditional methods have been based is that this was something relatively infrequent in a context of regular non-communicating worship. This is true alike of the Roman Catholic requirement of sacramental confession before Communion, of English Evangelical piety, and of the Scottish Presbyterian tradition, which virtually demanded a full-scale retreat before the quarterly sacrament. Now all of this is largely inapplicable to the recovery we are making in our generation of the pattern of the early Church, which saw the Eucharist as that in which the entire life and worship of the people of God *normally* centred on the Lord's Day—just as for the Plymouth Brethren the Breaking of Bread has always been *the* regular Sunday service. And our problem is how to take our full and personal part in *that*, not in infrequent individual acts of Communion, but in the regular common meal of the people of God.

The place perhaps from which to begin is the moment in the service that is actually called the Preparation. It is the moment when the bread and wine needed for the meal are separated and set apart from the rest. And as comment upon it in our manual stands the solemn reminder of St Augustine: 'There are *you* upon the table, there are *you* in the chalice.' The real question is, Are we in the deepest sense *prepared* to be there? Are we ready for this identification, and for what it will involve us in? Is the bread and wine so representative of our lives that we are wholly and willingly *there*, dedicated to what together we are to do and let Christ do to us? As a test we may place ourselves in turn within each of the four great acts of the Liturgy of which the bread and wine are the focus.

[1] A sermon preached at the College Communion on February 19, 1956.

First, are we really ready for the Offertory, for 'all (to quote our Communion manual again) that places us wholly at Christ's disposal—the offering of ourselves, our money, our prayers, our penitence'? There, straight away, are four heads under which we can examine ourselves. And of them let me single out one, the offering of our prayers. St Paul described the Liturgy at Corinth in these words: 'When you come together, each one has a hymn, a lesson, a revelation, a tongue, an interpretation'. Now *that* is live corporate worship, even if it was a bit chaotic; and I could wish that when you come together each of you had, at any rate a prayer, to add to the Offertory and be taken up in the great Intercession. And in this place there is every opportunity for making it articulate and asking us all to share in it—by means of the biddings and the box in the Ante-chapel which is there to receive them. Use this box as naturally as you use the alms-bag—so that the biddings may really come out of the heart of the congregation. Two years ago there was a period when the box was bursting and our worship nearly got as corybantic as that at Corinth. It is a sign that preparation is at a low ebb when not even one person has a prayer.

And then there is the second act, of Blessing, of sheer eucharistic joy which was such a mark of early Christian worship. Every Sunday is the first day of the week, a renewal of Easter. Do we come expectant, hurrying like the disciples to the empty tomb? Do we come prepared to lift up our hearts, to sing with the angels and archangels and all the company of heaven? Or do we come bleary, and resentful at being distracted from our pious slumbers, and loth even to stand up for the *Sursum Corda*?

Thirdly, the Breaking. There are *you* upon the Table. 'Sacrifice and offerings thou hast not desired, but a body hast thou prepared for me. . . . Then I said: "Lo, I come".' We come to Communion to be caught up into the sacrifice of Christ—to be broken with his body, to be dedicated to death for him. 'Are you able to drink the cup that I drink?' If we are to say we are able, we must be more prepared than were James and John.

And lastly, the Sharing. With this we reach that intensely personal moment upon which Communion preparation has traditionally tended to focus. 'Here I offer up to thee my soul; and thou offerest to me thy Son.' 'Lord, I am not worthy that thou shouldest come under my roof!' And yet it is not only for this individual act of communion that we must be ready. Am I prepared for the unconditional, unrestricted community which this act involves? Few things made so deep an impression on me in America as the discovery in a church I visited in the South that it was unthinkable for the negro verger to communicate with the whites at the table he tended. Such a congregation, like most of us, was not prepared for unrestricted community. But at any rate they did not share on Sundays the bread they would not eat together during the week, which might have been the greater hypocrisy. For being prepared for Communion is not only being prepared for a service in Chapel: it is being prepared for its unconditional community everywhere—on our College staircase, at home, in our social order. The bread we share here is not different: it is, quite deliberately, the bread we bring in from our daily lives, and, transformed, take back into them. There is no break, and the miracle of Christ does not destroy the substance or sever the connection. Consequently, preparation for Communion is not simply something done in Chapel or even in our rooms beforehand: it is everything that goes into the loaf and the cup we shall offer next Sunday.

But, having said all this, there is one last thing—the immediate corporate preparation which the Church itself provides in the Ante-Communion, or Liturgy of the Word. Learn to use the Ante-Communion, individually beforehand or corporately at the time, as a preparation for Communion. For it *is* this in two ways. First it holds up the standard—the law and the love of Christ—against which we must measure ourselves. Again, I would suggest using the help already offered in the Communion manual. Go through either the Ten Commandments or our Lord's summary of the Law under the four headings suggested—in our personal living, as a College community, in our national life, as members of a divided and embittered world—and there, if you want it, is a different form of self-examination for each week of term. And, secondly, the Ante-Communion puts into words, facet by facet, the meaning of the act that follows, as in the Upper Room Jesus prepared his disciples for the meaning of his death and promised presence. Take time to study beforehand the

Epistle and Gospel for the day, in a modern translation, and let them suggest the theme and intention of the week.

To close, I come back to where I started. We have to learn to prepare ourselves not for an isolated act, nor for an occasional one, nor for a purely individual one. Our task is rather so to integrate our lives that the whole action of the Liturgy becomes part of the very pattern and rhythm of our living. With this as the focus of our week and the centre of our community, everything we do is seen as preparation for Communion, of which the setting apart of the loaf on Sunday is but the climax. And equally everything we do becomes the outworking of Communion, of which the consecration of our bread on Sunday is but the sample and firstfruits of the rest.

III

THE COMMUNION MANUAL

THE HOLY
COMMUNION

*Receive therefore and eat the Body of Christ, you
who are already made members of Christ within the
Body of Christ. Take and drink the Blood of
Christ. Lest you should fall apart, drink that which
binds you together. Lest you should seem cheap
to yourselves, drink that which bought you. As
this when you eat and drink it, is changed into you,
so you are changed into the Body of Christ by an
obedient and holy life. You are receiving that which
(unless you receive unworthily) you have begun
to be. Make sure therefore that you do not eat
and drink judgement to yourselves. . . . He who
receives the mystery of unity, and does not preserve
the bond of peace, receives the mystery not for, but
against, himself.* ST AUGUSTINE

INTRODUCTION

The service of Holy Communion falls into two distinct parts, each with its own structure and centre.

The first part, the Liturgy of the Word, has its focus in the Bible, and takes place not at the Table but round the Lecterns. It is a service of prayer, Scripture-reading and preaching, in which the living Christ speaks to his assembled People, as Jesus discoursed with his disciples in the Upper Room, expounding the meaning of his death and promised presence.

In the second part, the Breaking of the Bread, he makes himself known in the Action which he instituted and which ever since has been the central act of the Church on the Lord's Day. In it he makes present to us, through the power of his risen life, all that he wrought on the Cross, till he comes in final victory.

The pattern of this action is four-fold, continuing that of Jesus at the Last Supper, when he took, and blessed, and broke, and gave.

We come, first, to commemorate with thanksgiving that he in his life, death and resurrection offered himself thus to be taken and consecrated, broken and given for us;

secondly, to trust his promise that in the bread and wine, taken, blessed, broken and shared as he commanded, he will come to us;

thirdly, to let our lives likewise be taken, blessed, broken and given in union with his, that God's redeeming work and rule may be extended through us.

For this second part the ministers take their places round the Table, after the manner of celebrating in the early Church. The presiding priest faces the people, flanked by the deacons and by the laymen who have offered the bread and the wine. The circle is completed by the congregation on whose behalf they minister in this concelebration of the whole People of God, in which each one of us has his liturgy to perform.

Come! Come! Lord Jesus, and stand in the midst of us, as thou didst stand in the midst of thy disciples. MOZARABIC MISSAL

SOME PRAYERS OF APPROACH

Jesus said:

I am the bread of life; he who comes to me shall not hunger, and he who believes in me shall never thirst.

ST JOHN vi. 35

Behold, I stand at the door and knock; if any one hears my voice and opens the door, I will come in to him and eat with him, and he with me.   REVELATION iii. 20

Cleanse our consciences, we beseech thee, O Lord, that thy Son, when he cometh, may find in us a dwelling-place prepared for himself.

Look graciously upon us, O Holy Spirit; and give us, for our hallowing, thoughts that pass into prayer, prayers that pass into love, and love that passes into life with thee for ever.

O Lord, have mercy on the sins of thy servants. May we banish from our minds all disunion and strife; may our souls be cleansed from all hatred and malice towards others; and may we receive the fellowship of the Holy Meal in oneness of mind and peace one with another.   LITURGY OF MALABAR

As watchmen look for the morning, so do we look for thee, O Christ. Come with the dawning of the day, and make thyself known to us in the breaking of the Bread; for thou art our God for ever and ever.

The Spirit and the Bride say, Come!
And he that hears, let him say, Come!
And he that is athirst, let him come;
He that will, let him take the water of life freely.
    Yea; I come quickly.
    Even so: Come, Lord Jesus!

REVELATION xxii. 17, 20

The opening Lord's Prayer formed originally part of the priest's private preparation. It is said quietly—out of the silence of the Father's family— that each one of us may through it make his own entrance into the holy of holies.

The ancient collect for purity now draws us together into the searching presence of God, whom we can worship worthily only as his own Spirit takes over our words and thoughts.

In our inarticulate groans the Spirit himself is pleading for us, and God who searches our inmost being knows what the Spirit means, because he pleads for God's own people in God's own way.

ROMANS viii. 26–7

For the cleansing of our hearts and the perfecting of our love we are brought up for measure
 not against someone else—
  of whom we can say, 'I am as good as he';
 not against our own best self—
  of whom we can say, 'That, and not my sin, is the true I';
 but against the absolute, holy love of God—
  before whom we can but repeat, 'Lord, have mercy!'

God's law examines us point by point
 in our personal living . . .
 as a College community . . .
 in our national standards . . .
 as members of a divided and embittered world . . .

first, in the place we give to God himself,

THE LITURGY OF THE WORD

The ministers enter, bearing the books from which the Word of God is to be read.

Then shall the priest begin:

THE LORD'S PRAYER

Our Father, which art in heaven, Hallowed be thy name; Thy kingdom come; Thy will be done; In earth as it is in heaven. Give us this day our daily bread. And forgive us our trespasses, As we forgive them that trespass against us. And lead us not into temptation; But deliver us from evil. Amen.

THE COLLECT FOR PURITY

Almighty God, unto whom all hearts be open, all desires known, and from whom no secrets are hid: Cleanse the thoughts of our hearts by the inspiration of thy Holy Spirit, that we may perfectly love thee, and worthily magnify thy holy name; through Christ our Lord. **Amen.**

Then shall follow, either:

THE TEN COMMANDMENTS

℣ God spake these words and said:
I am the Lord thy God; thou shalt have none other gods but me.

℟ **Lord, have mercy upon us, and incline our hearts to keep this law.**

℣ Thou shalt not make to thyself any graven image, nor the likeness of any thing that is in heaven above, or in the earth beneath, or in the water under the earth. Thou shalt not bow down to them, nor worship them.

℟ **Lord, have mercy upon us, and incline our hearts to keep this law.**

℣ Thou shalt not take the name of the Lord thy God in vain.

℟ **Lord, have mercy upon us, and incline our hearts to keep this law.**

then, in our attitude to others.

Christ's summary searches how deep, and how wide, our love really goes.

Love is patient; love is kind, and envies no one. Love is never boastful, nor conceited, nor rude; never selfish, never touchy. Love keeps no score of wrongs; it does not gloat over other men's sins, but exults in truth. There is nothing love cannot face; its faith and hope are boundless; its endurance knows no limits. I CORINTHIANS Xiii. 4–7

℣ Remember that thou keep holy the Sabbath day. Six days shalt thou labour, and do all that thou hast to do; but the seventh day is the Sabbath of the Lord thy God.

℟ **Lord, have mercy upon us, and incline our hearts to keep this law.**

℣ Honour thy father and thy mother.

℟ **Lord, have mercy upon us, and incline our hearts to keep this law.**

℣ Thou shalt do no murder.

℟ **Lord, have mercy upon us, and incline our hearts to keep this law.**

℣ Thou shalt not commit adultery.

℟ **Lord, have mercy upon us, and incline our hearts to keep this law.**

℣ Thou shalt not steal.

℟ **Lord, have mercy upon us, and incline our hearts to keep this law.**

℣ Thou shalt not bear false witness.

℟ **Lord, have mercy upon us, and incline our hearts to keep this law.**

℣ Thou shalt not covet.

℟ **Lord, have mercy upon us, and write all these thy laws in our hearts, we beseech thee.**

or:

OUR LORD'S SUMMARY OF THE LAW

℣ Our Lord Jesus Christ said:

Hear O Israel, The Lord our God is one Lord; and thou shalt love the Lord thy God with all thy heart, and with all thy soul, and with all thy mind, and with all thy strength. This is the first commandment.

And the second is like, namely this: Thou shalt love thy neighbour as thyself.

There is none other commandment greater than these. On these two commandments hang all the Law and the Prophets.

℟ **Lord, have mercy upon us, and incline our hearts to keep this law.**

Prayer for the Queen is often omitted here, being included later in the Intercession for the Church.

The white light of the Gospel is broken down, in the prism, as it were, of the Church's Year, so that week by week we may receive one bit of it and walk by it.

The Church's prayer for the week collects and focuses in its few words the countless prayers of the People of God throughout the world.

The Epistle is read out in the Christian community assembled for worship, as St Paul's letters were originally read. Occasionally it takes the form of a lesson from other parts of the New Testament, or even from the Old, a survival from the time when there were three readings—from the Prophets, the Apostles, and the Gospel.

A hymn divides the readings, as psalms and canticles did in the early Church.

The ministry of the Word comes to its climax in the Gospel, read by the deacon, to whom this special function is committed at his ordination: 'Take thou authority to read the Gospel in the Church of God.' For the words of Christ himself, as he speaks now to his People, we stand, and we address our response to him.

℣ Let us pray.

Here may be said one of the prayers for the Queen.

THE COLLECT OF THE DAY

℞ **Amen.**

The people being seated, a layman shall read:

THE EPISTLE

HYMN

All standing and turning to the lectern, the deacon shall announce the Gospel.

℞ **Glory be to thee, O Lord.**

THE GOSPEL

℞ **Praise be to thee, O Christ.**

In the words of the whole catholic Church, we take upon ourselves in affirmation and praise the great truths of the Faith just proclaimed to us.

> *I bind unto myself the name,*
> *The strong name of the Trinity;*
> *By invocation of the same,*
> *The Three in One, and One in Three,*
> *Of whom all nature hath creation;*
> *Eternal Father, Spirit, Word:*
> *Praise to the Lord of my salvation,*
> *Salvation is of Christ the Lord!*   ST PATRICK

The exposition and preaching of the Word is an integral part of the proclaiming of the Lord and his death in which the whole service consists.

Our response to Christ's Gospel takes expression in costing concern for his People and his Kingdom.

> *About the collection in aid of God's people . . . , every Sunday each of you is to put aside and keep by him a sum in proportion to his means.*
>   I CORINTHIANS xvi. 1-2
> *If anyone has this world's goods and sees his brother in need yet closes his heart against him, how does God's love dwell in him?*
>   I JOHN iii. 17

I believe in one God the Father Almighty, Maker of heaven and earth, And of all things visible and invisible:

And in one Lord Jesus Christ, the only-begotten Son of God, Begotten of his Father before all worlds, God of God, Light of Light, Very God of very God, Begotten, not made, Being of one substance with the Father, By whom all things were made: Who for us men, and for our salvation, came down from heaven, And was incarnate by the Holy Ghost of the Virgin Mary, And was made man, And was crucified also for us under Pontius Pilate. He suffered and was buried, And the third day he rose again according to the Scriptures, And ascended into heaven, And sitteth on the right hand of the Father. And he shall come again with glory to judge both the quick and the dead: Whose kingdom shall have no end.

And I believe in the Holy Ghost, The Lord, and giver of life, Who proceedeth from the Father and the Son, Who with the Father and the Son together is worshipped and glorified, Who spake by the Prophets. And I believe one Catholic and Apostolic Church. I acknowledge one Baptism for the remission of sins. And I look for the Resurrection of the dead, And the Life of the world to come. Amen.

THE SERMON

Then shall the deacon give out the Notices and announce the Collection.

In the opening Act is included all that places us wholly at Christ's disposal —the offering of ourselves, our money, our prayers, our penitence.

A new stage now begins. God's People is assembled for its most intimate action. Only those can share who are in real and deep unity, as the ancient Kiss of Peace at this point was a reminder. The Offertory sentences are from Psalms cxxxiii. 1 and xxvii. 6.

Jesus began by taking the loaf off the supper table. His work now, in us and through us, cannot start until the ordinary material of our lives, just as it is, is turned over entirely to him. In the Offertory we take a loaf baked in the College kitchens and a decanter of wine from the College cellars—symbols of our labour and our leisure, the gifts of God to us as we have worked upon them. They are brought up by laymen, out of the midst of our everyday life, and offered to God, together with our money.

An Offertory prayer formed a regular part of earlier liturgies. This is adapted from one in the Leonine Sacramentary, the oldest of the sources from which our collects come.

As the alms are taken back for their use in the world to which they have been given, the preparations are made for the Holy Meal. As the paten and the cup are handed to the president, we may recall the words of St Augustine to the newly confirmed: 'There are you upon the table, there are you in the chalice.'

THE BREAKING OF
THE BREAD

THE FIRST ACTION
TAKING

All remain standing.

THE OFFERTORY SENTENCES

℣ Behold, how good and joyful a thing it is, brethren, to dwell together in unity.

℟ **We will offer an oblation with great gladness, we will sing and speak praises unto the Lord.**

HYMN

The Bread and the Wine, together with the Alms, are taken up by representatives of the laity, and presented to the deacons, who place them upon the Holy Table.

Then shall the priest say:

THE OFFERTORY PRAYER

Receive, O Lord, we beseech thee, these gifts; accept in them the sacrifice of ourselves, and of thy mercy so perfect us, we pray, that we may be in life and death an offering to thee for ever; through Jesus Christ our Lord. **Amen.**

All kneel.

THE PREPARATION

The deacons set apart such of the Bread and Wine as shall be needed for the Communion.

A member of the congregation presents our local requests for prayer and thanksgiving, to be included in the intercession of the universal Church.

Intercession is one of the vital tasks laid upon us corporately as the worshipping Community. Spaces of silence are left, in which we may from week to week make each petition our own.

Thou who didst spread thy creating arms to the stars, strengthen our arms with power to intercede when we lift up our hands to thee.

ARMENIAN LITURGY

The introduction links the offering of our material gifts with our self-dedication in prayer to the needs of all mankind.

For the wholeness of the Church . . .

we offer ourselves in prayer.

For the rulers of the world; for our own Queen and nation; for peace and justice . . .

we offer ourselves in prayer.

For the ministry of the Church . . .

we offer ourselves in prayer.

92

Then shall a layman make:

THE BIDDINGS

After which the priest shall say:

THE INTERCESSION

Let us pray for the whole state of Christ's Church militant here in earth.

Almighty and everliving God, who by thy holy Apostle hast taught us to make prayers, and supplications, and to give thanks, for all men: We humbly beseech thee most mercifully to accept our alms and oblations, and to receive these our prayers, which we offer unto thy Divine Majesty;

Beseeching thee to inspire continually the universal Church with the spirit of truth, unity, and concord: And grant, that all they that do confess thy holy name may agree in the truth of thy holy Word, and live in unity, and godly love.

We beseech thee also to save and defend all Christian Kings, Princes, and Governors; and specially thy servant Elizabeth our Queen; that under her we may be godly and quietly governed: And grant unto her whole Council, and to all that are put in authority under her, that they may truly and impartially minister justice, to the punishment of wickedness and vice, and to the maintenance of thy true religion, and virtue.

Give grace, O heavenly Father, to all Bishops, Priests and Deacons, that they may both by their life and doctrine set forth thy true and living Word, and rightly and duly administer thy holy Sacraments.

For all the common People of God, and our own Christian community...

we offer ourselves in prayer.

For those throughout the world in distress, poverty, or sickness...

we offer ourselves in prayer.

With God's faithful servants of every age ...

we pray for his reign in us.

The presiding priest issues the invitation to draw near, reminding us that this sacrament unites us to Christ only as it unites us with his brethren.

A man must test himself before eating his share of the bread and drinking from the cup. For he who eats and drinks eats and drinks judgement on himself if he has no sense of the body. I CORINTHIANS xi. 28–9

For us there can be no terror in the Sacrament in so far as the Sacrament is Christ. But the Sacrament is also our brother who meets us there in Christ, our neighbour, our employer, our employee, our enemy. That is terrifying, because 'He who does not love his brother whom he has seen, cannot love God whom he has not seen'. M. A. C. WARREN

And to all thy people give thy heavenly grace; and specially to this congregation here present; that, with meek heart and due reverence, they may hear, and receive thy holy Word; truly serving thee in holiness and righteousness all the days of their life.

And we most humbly beseech thee of thy goodness, O Lord, to comfort and succour all them, who in this transitory life are in trouble, sorrow, need, sickness, or any other adversity.

And we also bless thy holy name for all thy servants departed this life in thy faith and fear; beseeching thee to give us grace so to follow their good examples, that with them we may be partakers of thy heavenly kingdom.

Grant this, O Father, for Jesus Christ's sake, our only Mediator and Advocate. **Amen.**

THE INVITATION

Ye that do truly and earnestly repent you of your sins, and are in love and charity with your neighbours, and intend to lead a new life, following the commandments of God, and walking from henceforth in his holy ways; Draw near with faith, and take this Holy Sacrament to your comfort; and make your humble confession to Almighty God, meekly kneeling upon your knees.

The bread and wine we have offered, our lives as they naturally are, are part of the old, sinful order. Before they and we can be united with the life of Jesus Christ in all its purity and power, we must be stripped down in utter penitence.

In this general confession we bring to God the fruits of our individual self-examination, and, particularly now, the short-comings of our corporate life as the Body of Christ in the College and the world, and the ways in which we personally have failed it and him.

I am the true vine, and my Father is the vinedresser. Every branch of mine that bears no fruit, he cuts away; and every branch that does bear fruit he cleans, that it may bear more fruit. You are made clean by the word which I have spoken to you. Abide in me, and I in you.

ST JOHN XV. 1–4

This is the message we have heard from him, that God is light and in him is no darkness at all. If we walk in the light, as he is in the light, we have fellowship with one another, and the blood of Jesus his Son cleanses us from all sin. If we confess our sins, he is faithful and just, and will forgive our sins and cleanse us from all unrighteousness.

I JOHN i. 5–9

Freed from the sin which binds us to earth, we prepare to take our place in heaven with Christ.

If then you have been raised with Christ, seek the things that are above, where Christ is, seated at the right hand of God. Set your minds on things that are above, not on things that are on the earth. For you have died, and your life is hid with Christ in God. COLOSSIANS iii. 1–3

THE CONFESSION

Almighty God, Father of our Lord Jesus Christ, Maker of all things, Judge of all men: We acknowledge and bewail our manifold sins and wickedness, Which we, from time to time, most grievously have committed, By thought, word and deed, Against thy Divine Majesty, Provoking most justly thy wrath and indignation against us. We do earnestly repent, And are heartily sorry for these our misdoings; The remembrance of them is grievous unto us; The burden of them is intolerable.

Have mercy upon us, Have mercy upon us, most merciful Father; For thy Son our Lord Jesus Christ's sake, Forgive us all that is past; And grant that we may ever hereafter Serve and please thee In newness of life, To the honour and glory of thy name; Through Jesus Christ our Lord. Amen.

THE ABSOLUTION

Almighty God, our heavenly Father, who of his great mercy hath promised forgiveness of sins to all them that with hearty repentance and true faith turn unto him: Have mercy upon you; pardon and deliver you from all your sins; confirm and strengthen you in all goodness; and bring you to everlasting life; through Jesus Christ our Lord. **Amen.**

THE GRACIOUS WORDS

Hear what comfortable words our Saviour Christ saith unto all that truly turn to him.

Come unto me all that travail and are heavy laden, and I will refresh you.

So God loved the world, that he gave his only-begotten Son, to the end that all that believe in him should not perish, but have everlasting life.

Hear also what Saint Paul saith.

This is a true saying, and worthy of all men to be received, That Christ Jesus came into the world to save sinners.

Hear also what Saint John saith.

If any man sin, we have an Advocate with the Father, Jesus Christ the righteous; and he is the propitiation for our sins.

The second Act is that from which the primitive title 'the Eucharist', or Thanksgiving, derives (as 'the Breaking of the Bread' and 'the Communion' come from emphasis on the third and fourth). It is an act of blessing, in which we bless God for all his gifts and above all for our redemption through Christ's death, and in which God blesses our gifts to become the means to us of Christ's resurrection life.

The note is set by the opening, and very ancient, dialogue of exultant thanksgiving, lifting us up to take our share, as part of the Church triumphant, in the ceaseless worship of the heavenly places.

After this, lo, a door was opened in heaven. And the voice which I had heard speaking to me like a trumpet, said, Come up hither! ... And behold, a great multitude which no man could number, from all tribes and peoples and tongues, standing before the throne and before the Lamb. ... And all the angels stood round the throne, and fell on their faces and worshipped God. ... And, day and night, they never cease to sing, Holy, holy, holy, is the Lord God Almighty, who was and is and is to come! REVELATION iv. 1, 8; vii. 9, 11

Then there was silence in heaven. REVELATION viii. 1

With the Sanctus still ringing in our ears, we pause, for a moment of corporate silence, to adore and to prepare.

Then I said, Woe is me! For my eyes have seen the King, the Lord of hosts! ISAIAH vi. 5

Conscious of our unworthiness of the terrible privilege to which we are called, that of sitting at table with Christ as an equal, of sharing his Food and drinking his Cup, we cast ourselves wholly on our Father's mercy.

Are you able to drink the cup that I drink? ... They said to him, We are able. ST MARK x. 38–9

Lord, I believe; help thou my unbelief. ST MARK ix. 24

THE SECOND ACTION
BLESSING

All stand.

THE SURSUM CORDA

℣ Lift up your hearts;

℟ **We lift them up unto the Lord.**

℣ Let us give thanks unto our Lord God;

℟ **It is meet and right so to do.**

THE PREFACE

It is very meet, right, and our bounden duty, that we should at all times, and in all places, give thanks unto thee, O Lord, Holy Father, Almighty, Everlasting God.

On festivals a proper preface follows.

Therefore with Angels and Archangels, and with all the company of heaven, we laud and magnify thy glorious name; evermore praising thee, and saying,

THE SANCTUS

Holy, holy, holy, Lord God of hosts, heaven and earth are full of thy glory. Glory be to thee, O Lord most High. Amen.

All kneel.

Then shall silence be kept for a space.

THE PRAYER OF HUMBLE ACCESS

Let us pray.

We do not presume to come to this thy Table, O merciful Lord, trusting in our own righteousness, but in thy manifold and great mercies. We are not worthy so much as to gather up the crumbs under thy Table. But thou art the same Lord, whose property is always to have mercy: Grant us therefore, gracious Lord, so to eat the Flesh of thy dear Son Jesus Christ, and to drink his Blood, that our sinful bodies may be made clean by his body, and our souls washed through his most precious Blood, and that we may evermore dwell in him, and he in us. Amen.

H

In this central prayer of the whole service, we commemorate with thanks-giving our perfect redemption through Christ; and pray that in its continuing power he will come among us now to transform our lives through his.

> Thy death, O Lord, we commemorate,
> Thy resurrection we confess,
> Thy coming we await!   FROM THE SOUTH INDIA LITURGY

The bread and wine of our world are redeemed and restored by Christ to carry his eternal life to men. 'This of yours', he says over our lives, 'this of you is my body and blood, my life.' In this act he gives to us his very self; and we ourselves are consecrated to be his Body, his People in the world.

The 'Amen' is the affirmation of praise that concludes the whole Act of Blessing, and the seal by which each one of us says, 'So be it, Lord; take and consecrate me'.

The life of God can be given, can be shared, only if it is broken and poured out. 'Unless a grain of wheat falls into the earth and dies, it remains alone' (St John xii. 24). That is the meaning of the Cross. We too, as his Body, can be used for bringing his life to the world only if we let ourselves be broken with him.

The deacons divide for distribution the Loaf which the presiding priest has just broken with the words and actions of Jesus. Breaking to share is the theme of the Fraction.

> The Lamb of God is broken and distributed, who being broken is not divided, but unites them who partake of him.
>   FROM THE LITURGY OF ST JOHN CHRYSOSTOM

> Be present, be present, O Jesus, thou good High Priest, as thou wast in the midst of thy disciples, and make thyself known to us in the breaking of the Bread.   SOUTH INDIA LITURGY

Almighty God, our heavenly Father, who of thy tender mercy didst give thine only Son Jesus Christ to suffer death upon the Cross for our redemption; who made there (by his one oblation of himself once offered) a full, perfect, and sufficient sacrifice, oblation, and satisfaction, for the sins of the whole world; and did institute, and in his holy Gospel command us to continue, a perpetual memory of that his precious death, until his coming again; Hear us, O merciful Father, we most humbly beseech thee; and grant that we receiving these thy creatures of bread and wine, according to thy Son our Saviour Jesus Christ's holy institution, in remembrance of his death and passion, may be partakers of his most blessed Body and Blood: who, in the same night that he was betrayed, took Bread; and when he had given thanks, he brake it, and gave it to his disciples, saying, Take, eat, this is my Body which is given for you: Do this in remembrance of me. Likewise after supper he took the Cup; and, when he had given thanks, he gave it to them, saying, Drink ye all of this; for this is my Blood of the New Testament, which is shed for you and for many for the remission of sins: Do this, as oft as ye shall drink it, in remembrance of me. **Amen.**

Then shall silence be kept for a space.

THE THIRD ACTION
BREAKING

THE FRACTION

As the priest hands the Loaf to the deacons to be broken, he may say:

The bread which we break, is it not a communion of the body of Christ? Because there is one loaf, we, who are many, are one body.

Then shall the deacons break the Bread.

Sharing in the one Loaf, we are recreated as the Body of Christ. The moment of climax is at once the most personal and the most corporate, as each of us individually partakes by faith in the Life we can know only as one.

We become one single body, limbs of his flesh and bone of his bone. This is the effect of the nourishment he gives us; he merges himself in us in order that we may be all one single thing, as one body, joined to one head. ST CHRYSOSTOM

The summons to Communion is from the Eastern Orthodox Liturgy and goes back to early Greek sources.

Let all mortal flesh keep silence, and with fear and trembling stand;
Ponder nothing earthly minded, for with blessing in his hand,
Christ our God to earth descendeth, our full homage to demand.
FROM THE LITURGY OF ST JAMES

Amen, my Lord and my God! O my Father, here I offer up to thee my soul; and thou offerest to me thy Son. What I offer is indeed an unclean habitation to receive the Holy One of Israel. Come in, nevertheless, thou Eternal Priest; but cleanse my house at thy coming. Come in, O Lord, with thy salvation, to a dying man, and make me whole. Come as thou didst to the publican. Oh, let this day salvation come to this house! DANIEL BREVINT (1616–95)

Since you are the body of Christ and his members, it is your mystery that is placed on the Lord's Table; it is your mystery that you receive. You hear the words: 'The body of Christ', and you answer 'Amen'. Be therefore members of Christ, that your 'Amen' may be true. . . . If you have received well, you are that which you have received.
ST AUGUSTINE

One in Christ, we join first in the family prayer of God's People, pledging our lives to his kingly rule.

THE FOURTH ACTION
SHARING

THE COMMUNION

The priest shall first himself communicate, with the deacons.

Then, as he hands the Bread and the Cup to the deacons for distribution to the people, he may say:

The things of God for the people of God!

Then shall the deacons deliver the Bread and the Cup to the people, saying:

The Body of our Lord Jesus Christ, which was given for thee, preserve thy body and soul unto everlasting life. Take and eat this in remembrance that Christ died for thee, and feed on him in thy heart by faith with thanksgiving.

The blood of our Lord Jesus Christ, which was shed for thee, preserve thy body and soul unto everlasting life. Drink this in remembrance that Christ's Blood was shed for thee, and be thankful.

THE LORD'S PRAYER

Our Father, **which art in heaven, Hallowed be thy name; Thy kingdom come; Thy will be done; In earth as it is in heaven. Give us this day our daily bread. And forgive us our trespasses, As we forgive them that trespass against us. And lead us not into temptation; But deliver us from evil: For thine is the kingdom, The power, and the glory, For ever and ever. Amen.**

Caught up into the sacrifice of his Son, we yield ourselves in gratitude to God, no longer simply as ourselves but as members of Christ, to be used as God's instrument in the world.

> *I am no longer my own, but thine.*
> *Put me to what thou wilt, rank me with whom thou wilt;*
> *Put me to doing, put me to suffering;*
> *Let me be employed for thee or laid aside for thee,*
> *   exalted for thee or brought low for thee;*
> *Let me be full, let me be empty;*
> *Let me have all things, let me have nothing;*
> *I freely and heartily yield all things to thy pleasure and disposal.*
> *And now, O glorious and blessed God,*
> *   Father, Son and Holy Spirit,*
> *Thou art mine, and I am thine. So be it.*
>   JOHN WESLEY. THE METHODIST COVENANT SERVICE

We thank God for having renewed us as the Body of Christ and given us this pledge of his coming Reign;

and we pray that we may now go on, and go out, in the strength of this Fellowship.

Then shall be said, either:

THE PRAYER OF OBLATION

O Lord and heavenly Father, we thy humble servants entirely desire thy fatherly goodness mercifully to accept this our sacrifice of praise and thanksgiving; most humbly beseeching thee to grant, that by the merits and death of thy Son Jesus Christ, and through faith in his blood, we and all thy whole Church may obtain remission of our sins, and all other benefits of his passion.

And here we offer and present unto thee, O Lord, ourselves, our souls and bodies, to be a reasonable, holy, and living sacrifice unto thee; humbly beseeching thee, that all we, who are partakers of this Holy Communion, may be fulfilled with thy grace and heavenly benediction.

And although we be unworthy, through our manifold sins, to offer unto thee any sacrifice, yet we beseech thee to accept this our bounden duty and service; not weighing our merits, but pardoning our offences, through Jesus Christ our Lord; by whom, and with whom, in the unity of the Holy Ghost, all honour and glory be unto thee, O Father Almighty, world without end. **Amen.**

or:

THE PRAYER OF THANKSGIVING

Almighty and everliving God, we most heartily thank thee, for that thou dost vouchsafe to feed us, who have duly received these holy mysteries, with the spiritual food of the most precious Body and Blood of thy Son our Saviour Jesus Christ; and dost assure us thereby of thy favour and goodness towards us; and that we are very members incorporate in the mystical body of thy Son, which is the blessed company of all faithful people; and are also heirs through hope of thy everlasting kingdom, by the merits of the most precious death and passion of thy dear Son.

And we most humbly beseech thee, O heavenly Father, so to assist us with thy grace, that we may continue in that holy fellowship, and do all such good works as thou hast prepared for us to walk in; through Jesus Christ our Lord, to whom, with thee and the Holy Ghost, be all honour and glory, world without end. **Amen.**

All is now gathered up in a final burst of praise and plea for help. The words of the early Christian hymn link our worship with the angels' song at the birth of the Prince of Peace, and send us forth in the power of him who even now is taking away the sin of the world and reigns as its rightful Lord.

Finished and perfected, O Christ our God, so far as in us lies, is the mystery which thou hast ordained. We have made the memorial of thy death, we have seen the symbol of thy resurrection, we have been filled with thine inexhaustible bounty, and enriched with thine undying life; and of this do thou vouchsafe to count us all worthy in the world to come. LITURGY OF ST BASIL

The sharing of bread, concluded now sacramentally, must be continued socially—and thence economically and politically.

When we come together to break bread, we must break it to the hungry, to God himself in his poor members. H. L'ESTRANGE (1659)

This prayer, from The Didache, was probably actually used at the primitive Christian Agape, or Love Feast.

GLORIA IN EXCELSIS

Glory be to God on high, **and in earth peace, good will towards men.** We praise thee, we bless thee, we worship thee, we glorify thee, we give thanks to thee for thy great glory, O Lord God, heavenly King, God the Father Almighty.

O Lord, the only-begotten Son Jesu Christ; O Lord God, Lamb of God, Son of the Father, that takest away the sins of the world, have mercy upon us. Thou that takest away the sins of the world, have mercy upon us. Thou that takest away the sins of the world, receive our prayer. Thou that sittest at the right hand of God the Father, have mercy upon us.

For thou only art holy; thou only art the Lord; thou only, O Christ, with the Holy Ghost, art most high in the glory of God the Father. Amen.

All kneel.

THE BLESSING

The peace of God, which passeth all understanding, keep your hearts and minds in the knowledge and love of God, and of his Son Jesus Christ our Lord: and the blessing of God Almighty, the Father, the Son, and the Holy Ghost, be amongst you and remain with you always. **Amen.**

HYMN

The ministers go out, a deacon carrying the remainder of the Loaf not set apart for the Communion, to be shared at the Breakfast.

At the Breakfast this prayer shall be said:

As this bread that is broken was scattered as grain upon the mountains and, gathered together, became one; so let thy Church be gathered from the ends of the earth into thy Kingdom, for thine is the glory and the power through Christ our Lord. **Amen.**

SOME PRAYERS OF THANKSGIVING
AND DEDICATION

WHICH MAY BE USED AFTER COMMUNICATING
OR AT THE CLOSE OF THE SERVICE

Praise the Lord, O my soul,
    and all that is within me praise his holy name.
Praise the Lord, O my soul,
    and forget not all his benefits;
Who forgiveth all thy sin,
    and healeth all thine infirmities;
Who saveth thy life from destruction,
    and crowneth thee with mercy and loving-kindness;
Who satisfieth thy mouth with good things,
    making thee young and lusty as an eagle.   PSALM ciii. 1–5

From glory to glory advancing, we praise thee, O Lord;
    Thy name with the Father and Spirit be ever adored.
From strength unto strength we go forward on Sion's highway,
    To appear before God in the city of infinite day.
Thanksgiving, and glory and worship, and blessing and love,
    One heart and one song have the saints upon earth and above.
Evermore, O Lord, to thy servants thy presence be nigh;
    Ever fit us by service on earth for thy service on high.
                  FROM THE LITURGY OF ST JAMES

Strengthen, O Lord, the hands which have been held out to
    receive thy Holy Things.
Grant that the ears which have heard the voice of thy songs
        may be closed to the voice of clamour and dispute;
      that the eyes which have seen thy great love
        may also behold thy blessed hope;
      that the tongues which have sung the Sanctus
        may also speak the truth;
      that the feet which have trodden thy courts
        may ever walk in the light;
      that the bodies which have tasted thy living Body
        may be restored to newness of life.
                    LITURGY OF MALABAR

O Lord, thou hast come into our hearts:
Help us to carry thy love into the world.
   Where there is hate, may we bring love;
   Where there is offence, may we bring pardon;
   Where there is error, may we bring truth;
   Where there is doubt, may we bring faith;
   Where there is despair, may we bring hope;
   Where there is darkness, may we bring light;
   Where there is sadness, may we bring joy.
O Lord, thou hast given thyself for us:
Help us, as we go out into the world,
   not to seek our own comfort, but to console others;
   not to demand to be understood, but to understand others;
   not to insist on being loved, but to love others.
For it is in giving that we receive thy gifts;
   It is in forgetting ourselves that we find thee;
   It is in pardoning others that we are forgiven;
   It is in dying that we are raised to life eternal.

FROM ST FRANCIS

O Lord, who hast called us to be thy witnesses, cleanse us from all unbelief and sloth, and fill us with hope and zeal; that we may do thy work, and bear thy cross, and bide thy time, and see thy glory.

When you reflect after Communion, 'What have I done to-day?', say to yourself, 'I have done more than on any busiest day of the week. I have yielded myself to take part with the Church in Christ's finished Act of Redemption, which is greater than the making of the world.' P. T. FORSYTH

The Word was made flesh, and dwelt among us (and we beheld his glory, the glory as of the only-begotten of the Father), full of grace and truth. ST JOHN i. 14

Thanks be to God for his unspeakable gift!